The Logic of the Revelation of St. John

The Logic of The Revelation of St. John

STEPHEN BEEBE

Bahá'í Publishing Trust
New Delhi, India

Copyright © Stephen Beebe

First Edition 1998 (August)
Reprint March 2001

ISBN : 81-86953-34-5

Published by Bahá'í Publishing Trust
F-3/6, Okhla Industrial Area, Phase - I
NEW DELHI- 110 020, India

Printed by : Greatway Prints

*This work is dedicated to
the memory of the Imám Ḥusayn
whose story of sacrifice adorns
the pages of Revelation*

Acknowledgements

The author wishes to thank Mr. Donald Witzell for his revision of the content of this book in its original text in Spanish; Mrs. Francia Valcarcel for the revision of the Spanish grammar, spelling and expression; Mrs. Truella Hicks for assisting in the translation from Spanish into English, and without whose enthusiasm this task would never have been accomplished; and his family for having sacrificed many hours that we would otherwise have spent together, while this book was being completed.

Contents

1. The Fascination of Revelation — 1
2. Analysis of the Seven Stages — 7
3. Progressive Revelation — 18
4. Stages I to IV — 23
5. The Remaining Three Stages — 30
6. Chapter 11 of Revelation: The Two Witnesses — 55
7. The Fifth Stage — 60
8. The Sixth Stage — 64
9. The Seventh Stage — 74
10. The Two Prophets of the Modern Epoch — 79
11. The Remaining Chapters of Revelation: Analysis — 94
12. Chapter 12 of Revelation: The Woman and the Beast — 101
13. Chapters 17 to 19: The Harlot and her Judgement — 105
14. Chapters 20 to 22: The Millennium; the New Jerusalem — 114
15. Chapter 13: The Two Beasts — 142
16. Chapter 14: The Harvest of the Vineyard — 146
17. The Throne of God; the Lamb and the 144,000 — 150

18. Armageddon 176
19. A Miniature Book of Revelation: Matthew 24 181
Conclusion: 195
Appendix 1: Other Biblical Prophecies Fulfilled in the Modern Era 204
Appendix 2: Bibliography: 210
Glossary 212

Chapter 1
The Fascination of Revelation

I think that few books of whatever age, of whatever size or theme, have motivated so much curiosity and controversy as the Book of Revelation. Theologians have defended it as the Word of God, skeptics have scorned it as mythology, historians have interpreted it as symbolic history of the primitive church in its struggle to survive.

While all the Bible has been the object of vivid controversy, Revelation has a special fascination that has intrigued Christians for centuries, specifically for two reasons.

First, the contents of Revelation are particularly mysterious: the images of unknown worlds; the glory of angels and the terror of dreadful beasts; the City of God and the pit burning with sulphur, the holy people of God and the sinners condemned to hell. All its themes are alien to anything that we have seen or known, and still, we accept them as divine revelation of the Truth. The act of believing in something so vivid and at the same time so mysterious stimulates the curiosity and creates a great desire to understand it better.

Second, since such visions represent prophecies of events to come, an expectation is created of things anticipated but little understood, resulting in an anxiety about the future. It is this combination of anxiety and curiosity that has made Revelation the greatest unknown and the most fascinating book of the Bible.

Revelation represents only 6% of the New Testament and less than 2% of the entire Bible, yet its impact over Western culture has been disproportionately great. Its images have penetrated our consciousness and we find them in art, literature and movies. Persons who have never read Revelation are acquainted with references to its content: the four horsemen that are to bring destruction to the world; the beast whose number is 666; and the battle of Armageddon. For example, the Apocalyptic predictions of the end of the world are implanted so deeply in our subconscious that the modern threat of nuclear war seems to be the natural fulfillment of such predictions.

It is ironic, however, that a book which has had such a great influence, has been the object of so many doubts over its veracity. One author notes that over the centuries, Revelation "has been alternately banned and accepted numberless times. It is still excluded from the Bible of the Greek Orthodox Church."[1]

Many modern experts study Revelation in the historical context of the primitive church, and consider that it was written in response to the persecutions of the Church by the Roman Empire.

The Fascination of Revelation

Its purpose, therefore, would have been to encourage the early Christians and to assure them of the imminent defeat of Rome. According to this interpretation, Rome is represented as the harlot in Chapter 17, seated upon the seven mountains. This point of view, which interprets Revelation only in terms of the immediate conditions of the primitive church, denies in a sense the orthodox interpretation that the visions constitute divine revelation of future events and the return of Christ.

There is even doubt among scholars concerning who the author of Revelation was. While traditionally it is supposed that John, the Apostle of Christ, was the same John of Revelation and the only author, some modern experts suggest that Revelation is a collection of writings of many authors.

While some doubt the divine origin of the book, those who accept its authenticity are in complete disagreement over its meaning. For example, Revelation is the origin of the doctrine of the millennium, the expected reign of peace that is to endure 1,000 years, when the Government of Christ and His resurrected saints will be imposed. As a result of the hopes engendered by this prophecy, numerous sects have come into being, each with a different interpretation of the manner in which the millennium will come.

Most Christians believe that Christ will come to initiate the millennium, and that the millennium will be the work of Christ Himself. However, a minority believe that the second coming will occur after the millennium and will be the dramatic climax of the 1,000 years. This minority sustains that the millennium will be established by the efforts of men inspired by the Evangels. In contrast with these interpretations, the Church of the Middle Ages taught that the millennial reign will never exist in this world, but that Revelation is rather an allegory of the struggle between good and evil; between the spiritual world and the material world. According to this point of view, any person could gain the Kingdom of God spiritually in his mystic communion with God.

In regard to the manner of interpreting the prophecies, some say that the prophecies are symbolic, and others insist that they must be fulfilled literally. Plentiful are the interpretations, but these are for the most part arbitrary, since each individual assigns meanings according to his own understanding, whim, or prejudice. For example, some sects consider that the saints mentioned in Revelation represent their own faithful to the exclusion of other Christians. Others interpret the great beast as another sister church with whose doctrine they are not in agreement. We can well ask ourselves, is it possible to attain to a truly objective interpretation? In view of so much controversary, what can we conclude about Revelation? Is it purely allegorical of the struggle between good and evil? Or does it predict specific events in history? Is it symbolic or literal? Is it past or future?

The present work assumes the position that Revelation is of divine origin, that it is in great part prophetic, and that its visions represent historical events. This work is one more attempt to unravel the mysteries that lie hidden in the Book of Revelation.

Starting from this position, how can we gain an interpretation of Revelation which is less arbitrary and more accurate? If we are to draw nearer to a true understanding of Revelation, we must first analyze its contents, free from prejudices, before we interpret them. Even in the study of Revelation we can apply the so called "scientific method", first analyzing the facts objectively, later formulating an hypothesis to explain them, and finally testing this hypothesis, whether it be by means of experimentation or by a more critical and extensive comparison with the facts, in order to accept or reject it. This study attempts to separate the processes of analysis and interpretation, seeking first to gain an objective analysis, and only then to enter the phase of interpretation. The following chapter will be dedicated to this analysis.

We can compare Revelation with a picture puzzle whose pieces are scattered and jumbled. If we fix our attention on each isolated piece, we will not be able to understand the meaning of the whole puzzle, and if we try to guess its significance looking only at the pieces, we will surely make mistakes. First we have to organize and put the pieces together in order to grasp the overall picture, and once this is done, we can understand the significance and role of individual pieces. If we follow this method of analysis, we will find patterns that will reveal to us the meanings of the Book of Revelation and that will open to us its mysteries.

REFERENCES

1. Elena Maria Marsella, *The Quest for Eden*, pp. 203-4.

CHAPTER 2

Analysis of the Seven Stages

A rapid perusal of Revelation shows us that the number "7" has a special role in the narrative. Numerology enthusiasts might attribute a mystical power or a transcendental meaning to the number, but for the present we will limit ourselves to describing events which occur in groups of seven. Specifically we find the following:
1. There are 7 letters addressed to 7 ancient churches (Chapters 2-3).
2. There is a book sealed with 7 seals which are opened one at a time (Chapters 5 to 7).
3. There are 7 angels with 7 trumpets that are sounded one by one (Chapters 8 to 11).
4. There are 7 angels with 7 plagues, in the form of 7 vials filled with the wrath of God, which are poured out over the earth one at a time (Chapters 15 to 16).

At times some stage in a series of 7 events is described in greater detail and sometimes there are accounts of visions inserted in the midst of a series of seven.

What is the significance of the grouping of events by sevens? Before we answer this question it is interesting to make a comparison of Revelation with the book of Genesis. As we know, Genesis also has a narrative in seven stages which constitutes the story of creation. Some maintain that this account should be understood literally, and others believe that it has a symbolic meaning. Those who incline toward a symbolic interpretation cite the evidence that, according to the story, the sun was not created until the fourth day, therefore there was no way of marking the first three days. This suggests, they say, that the days of creation represent something more than days of the calendar. But we will not dwell upon this point at this time. What interests us is to make a comparison between Genesis and Revelation; between the 7 days of creation, the 7 letters to the churches, the 7 seals, the 7 trumpets, and the 7 plagues.

In Table 1 is a summary of some of the content from Genesis and from Revelation to facilitate comparisons. The first column represents the creation story of Genesis, with the events of the seven successive days, and the other columns represent the events related to Revelation. The reader should familiarize himself with Table 1 and compare it with the Biblical text to be able to understand the study which follows.

Analysis of the Seven Stages

TABLE 1
A Summary of Some Events of Genesis and Revelation

GENESIS		REVELATION		
The 7 Days of creation	7 letters to 7 churches	A book with 7 seals	7 angels with 7 trumpets	7 angels with 7 plagues
1. The first light	-Ephesus -A fall -Tree of Life midst Paradise of God	-A white horse	-Hail, fire, blood upon the earth -A crown	-Plague on men with sign of the beast
2. Sea covers everything -Creation of heaven	-Smyrna -Tribulation	-A red horse -Kills with sword	-1/3 of sea becomes blood -Death	-Sea becomes blood -Death
3. Sea is separated fountains from dry	-Pergamos -Doctrine of Balaam -Hidden manna	-A black horse -A balance	-1/3 of rivers and fountains bitter	-Rivers and fountains become blood
4. Sun, moon, stars created	-Thyatira -Charity, service, faith, patience -Power over nations	-A pale horse -Death -Power over ¼ of the earth	-Sun, moon, and stars injured	-Sun burns men
5. Creation of fish and fowls	-Sardis -White raiment for saints	-Martyrs receive white robes	-1st Woe -A star falls -Smoke from abyss darkens sun	-Plague on the seat of beast -Darkness
6. Creation of man and beasts	-Philadelphia -An open door -Jews will come -I come quickly -Promise of New Jerusalem	-A great earthquake -Sun is darkened -The heaven is departed -The powerful hide from the Lamb	-2nd Woe -4 angels loosed from Euphrates -2 witnesses -Earthquake -3rd Woe comes quickly	-Plague on Euphrates -Call to Armageddon -I come as a thief
7. Rest Day of the Lord	-Laodicea -I am at the door and call -Faithful share the throne	-Silence in heaven -Thunder, voices, lightning, earthquake	-3rd Woe -Kingdom of God -24 elders before the throne -Judgement and recompense -Lightning, voices, thunder, earthquakes	-Lightning, voices, thunder earthquake -Judgement of Babylon

What do we find upon comparing each stage across columns?

The First Stage

In the first stage we see the following: on the first day of creation the light was brought into being; the letter to the first church, that of Ephesus, which speaks of Paradise and of the Tree of Life; the first seal is broken and a white horse appears; the first trumpet sounds and hail and fire fall from heaven; and with the first plague a sore appears upon the worshipers of a beast. No relation is evident between the events of the first stage.

The Second Stage

On the second day of Genesis, we find a division of the waters to form the heavens:

"And God said, Let there be a firmament in the midst of the waters: and let it divide the waters from the waters." (Gen. 1:6)

In other words, on this day all existence was surrounded by water; the sea still covered all of the earth.

Upon sounding the second trumpet, there is also an allusion to the sea:

"And the second angel sounded, and as it were a great mountain burning with fire was cast into the sea: and the third part of the sea become blood; And the third part of the creatures which were in the sea, and had life, died; ..." (Rev. 8:8-9)

With the second cup of the wrath of God, we read something similar:

Analysis of the Seven Stages

"And the second angel poured out his vial upon the sea: and it became as the blood of a dead man; and every living soul died in the sea," (Rev. 16:3)

Upon opening the second seal of the book, we see a red horse (like blood) and there is death:

"And there went out another horse that was red: and power was given to him that sat thereon to take peace from the earth, and that they should kill one another...." (Rev. 6:4)

Here in the second stage there appears that there is a certain relationship between columns. In particular, references are repeated to the SEA, to BLOOD, and to DEATH. What does this relationship mean? Do we find any relationship in the following stages also?

The Third Stage

Here we find more references to water. On the third day of Genesis, the water is separated from the land:

"And God said, Let the waters under the heaven be gathered together unto one place, and let the dry land appear: and it was so." (Gen. 1:9)

With the third trumpet, the waters of the RIVERS and FOUNTAINS became bitter:

"And the third angel sounded, and there fell a great star from heaven, burning as it were a lamp, and it fell upon the third part of the rivers, and upon the fountains of waters... and many men died of the

waters, because they were made bitter."
(Rev. 8:10-11)

Something similar happens when the third vial of wrath is poured out:

"And the third angel poured out his vial upon the rivers and fountains of waters: and they became blood." (Rev. 16:4)

Again we see a relationship across columns in the third stage. There is more mention of WATER, especially to RIVERS and FOUNTAINS.

The Fourth Stage

The fourth day of Genesis is the day in which the SUN, the MOON, and the STARS are created. (Gen. 1:16)

Upon sounding the fourth trumpet, there is mention of the SUN, the MOON, and the STARS:

"And the fourth angel sounded, and the third part of the SUN was smitten, and the third part of the MOON, and the third part of the STARS;..." (Rev. 8:12)

With the fourth plague, there is also mention of the SUN:

"And the fourth angel poured out his vial upon the SUN; and power was given unto him to scorch men with fire." (Rev. 16:8)

The celestial bodies seem to have some special relationship with the fourth stage.

Furthermore, in the fourth stage a promise of earthly power is repeated twice.

In the letter to the church of Thyatira, we read:

"And he that overcometh, and keepeth my works unto the end, to him will I give

Analysis of the Seven Stages

POWER OVER THE NATIONS" (Rev. 2:26)

And upon opening the fourth seal of the Book, a pale horse appears and to the horse and its rider:

"...POWER· was given unto them over the fourth part of the EARTH,..." (Rev. 6:8)

The Fifth Stage

What points do we find in common across columns of the fifth stage?

First, there is a promise to clothe the saints in WHITE RAIMENT. In the letter to the fifth Church, we read:

"He that overcometh, the same shall be clothed in WHITE RAIMENT;... (Rev. 3:5)

And when the fifth seal is opened, we also read of WHITE ROBES:

"And when he had opened the fifth seal, I saw under the altar the souls of them that were slain for the word of God, and for the testimony which they held: ...And WHITE ROBES were given to every one of them..." (Rev. 6:9-11)

Also, the fifth stage is a time of great darkness:

"And the fifth angel sounded, ...and there arose a smoke out of the pit, as the smoke of a great furnace; and the sun and the air were DARKENED by reason of the smoke of the pit" (Rev. 9:1-2)

"And the fifth angel poured out his vial upon the seat of the beast; and his kingdom was full of DARKNESS." (Rev. 16:10)

Darkness on one side and martyrs with white robes on the other, these are the signs of the fifth stage.

The Sixth Stage

This is a stage of many great events - among them the following:

> "And I beheld when he had opened the sixth seal, and lo, there was a GREAT EARTHQUAKE" (Rev. 6:12)

Again we read of a destructive GREAT EARTHQUAKE after the sounding of the sixth trumpet:

> "And the same hour was there a GREAT EARTHQUAKE, and the tenth part of the city fell, and in the earthquake were slain of men seven thousand:" (Rev. 11:13)

Also in this stage we find the only two references in Revelation to the River Euphrates:

> "And the sixth angel sounded, and I heard a voice....saying to the sixth angel which had the trumpet, Loose the four angels which are bound in the great RIVER EUPHRATES; ... (Rev. 2:13-14)

> And the sixth angel poured out his vial upon the great RIVER EUPHRATES;.... (Rev. 16:12)

Conclusion: The sixth stage has a relationship with the region around the River Euphrates, where there would be a great earthquake.

The Seventh Stage

LIGHTNING, THUNDER, VOICES, AND EARTHQUAKES. This is a very specific

Analysis of the Seven Stages

combination of signs; however, precisely this combination is repeated three times in relation to the seventh stage:

"And when he had opened the seventh seal, there was silence in heaven about the space of half an hour... and there were VOICES, and THUNDERINGS, and LIGHTNINGS, and an EARTHQUAKE.." (Rev. 8:1-5)

"And the seventh angel sounded ... And the temple of God was opened in heaven, and there was seen in his temple the ark of his testament; and there were LIGHTNINGS, and VOICES, and THUNDERINGS, and an EARTHQUAKE, and great hail" (Rev. 11:15-19)

"And the seventh angel poured out his vial into the air; ... And there were VOICES, and THUNDERS, and LIGHTNINGS; and there was a great EARTHQUAKE, such as was not since men were upon the earth, so mighty an earthquake, and so great." (Rev. 16:17-18)

However, that which is even more noteworthy in the seventh stage is the repetition of a theme: judgement and chastisement on one hand, and peace and recompense on the other. With the seventh trumpet the dead will be judged and with the seventh plague Babylonia will be chastised. In the seventh stage the kingdoms of the earth will belong to God. All these are traditionally considered to be central themes of Revelation and they have a special relationship with the seventh stage.

Also, this theme has a relationship with the seventh day of creation on which God rested. The seventh stage is a stage of peace and rest for the nations of the world, after the judgement and chastisement.

What do these observations of the seven stages suggest to us? The implication of these relationships is that each series of seven events is a repetition of the same seven events. That is, the seven days of creation, the seven churches mentioned in Revelation, the book with seven seals, etc., all are symbolic of one single theme which is repeated many times in a cyclic fashion. We will test this hypothesis in the interpretation phase of our study.

But first, what other evidence is there that Revelation is written as a repetitive and cyclic narrative? If we consider the events of Revelation, we see that it is impossible that they occur in the order in which they are written. In Chapter 6 we read that the sun, the moon, and the heavens were rolled up, that is, that the celestial bodies disappear. Further on, in Chapter 8, the sun, moon, and stars are mentioned again, although supposedly they no longer exist. This can be explained if we suppose that the events are NOT written in a strictly chronological sequence. A repetitive and cyclic format, as we have described, can explain this apparent inconsistency. We will see throughout this study that a key for understanding Revelation is the recognition that it is not written in chronological order. The same seven stages which we have described will help us to organize the other events in a logical order.

Analysis of the Seven Stages

Up to this point we have not attempted to interpret any passage of Revelation. We have only analyzed a part of the content of the book, identifying certain relationships which exist and suggesting a general explanation for these relationships. But the question remains: What is the significance of the seven events repeated in different forms and with different symbolic expressions? Is there an explanation which can take into account and harmonize all of these forms of expression, and thus justify what we have suggested, that is, that each series of seven events is symbolic of one common theme? We offer this explanation in the following section.

CHAPTER 3

Progressive Revelation

There is a religious doctrine which will be of great use for our study, which is known as "Progressive Revelation"[1]. According to this doctrine, the Revelation of God has not been absolute nor "once for all times". On the contrary, God has revealed Himself to His children gradually through a long series of Prophets, each of them bringing a message that was adequate for His own age.

For example, in an age when man lived in a primitive pastoral society, God spoke to him through Abraham. From the Message of Abraham, His example of faith in the one God has survived until our time. Years later, Moses established the Law, which represented a great advance over any former Revelation. The Law was a strict and necessary discipline for the Israelites, recently liberated from slavery in Egypt. By the means of the Law, the Israelites gained a high level of social development for that age of history. When Jesus came, He chose to leave some of the Laws of Moses intact while others, such as the law of divorce, were modified. From this example, we must suppose that:

1. Jesus had authority to act in this manner.

Progressive Revelation

2. It was according to the wisdom of God to change such laws in that age.

Jesus spoke of love toward one's neighbor and His Message was adequate for a people who had already abandoned the nomadic life and lived in cities. Just as the Mosaic Law was revealed to fulfill the needs of the Israelites in the time of Moses, the Message of Jesus was given to satisfy the needs of another age.

If we consider the succession of Prophets and their respective Messages from Abraham to Moses and from Moses to Jesus, we see a process of change, growth and progress, both spiritual and social. This succession of Prophetic messages is known as "Progressive Revelation" and is considered to be the cause of the progress of mankind.

The succession of Prophets began with Adam and was continued with Noah, Moses, and other Founders of the great religions of the world. Each one of these Prophets occupies a station above other human beings, a station which we call the "Holy Spirit". In their spiritual essence, all of the Prophets are the same and only differ in their Missions and Messages - which are adapted to the needs of humanity in a given epoch.

Each Prophet opens a new epoch in the history of mankind and each one is the Lord of His respective age. With the coming of each Prophet, the laws of the previous Dispensation are effectively abrogated and the Prophet has the authority to renew the previous laws or to formulate totally new ones, because each Prophet is as a Divine Physician, who prescribes spiritual teachings according to the particular illnesses of His time. But as to His own knowledge, His essence, His spiritual station, each one is as the others, each one is a channel for the one Holy Spirit (or in the terminology of the New Testament, the Spirit of Christ, which is the Messianic Spirit). The following words of Peter testify to the truth of the above:

> "...For the prophecy came not in old time by the will of man: but holy men of God spake as they were moved by the Holy Ghost." (2 Peter 2:21)
>
> "Of which salvation the prophets have inquired and searched diligently, who prophesied of the grace that should come unto you: Searching what, or what manner of time the Spirit of Christ which was in them did signify,...." (1 Peter 1:10, 11)

From these verses we understand that the Spirit of Christ is the same Holy Spirit and that this Spirit is eternal and has always been the source of guidance for humanity through the channel of God's Prophets, whether Noah, Moses, Abraham, or Jesus.

What significance has this doctrine for interpreting the seven events which are repeated in Genesis and Revelation?

We suggest that the seven events represent seven stages in the spiritual development of humanity and that each stage is related to one of the Prophets. From this point of view, the seven days of creation are not days of material creation but of spiritual creation, that is, the progressive and spiritual evolution of mankind.

Likewise, the seven Churches of Asia are not seven Christian communities of the ancient world. If that were the case, why are only seven named, when in the time of the Apostles there already existed many more? And why only in Asia, when there were also communities in Europe? Furthermore, all of these communities have been outside the domain of Christianity for centuries and some of the cities are totally non-existent[2], even though their churches were given promises for the last days.

Rather the seven Churches of Asia represent seven RELIGIONS born in Asia, because all the principle religions that exist in the world today had their beginnings in Asia.

What does the book with the seven seals represent? The book represents the knowledge of God. The Prophets have come successively and have revealed, each in His time, another measure of the knowledge of God and a new chapter in religion. The act of opening a seal represents yet another revelation of divine knowledge.

The seven angels with trumpets represent seven Prophets. The trumpet represents the voice of the Prophet, that is to say, His Word and His call to humanity. Thus it says in Rev. 1:10: "..I...heard behind me a great voice, as of a trumpet."

The seven plagues are also part of the seven Progressive Revelations, because the Prophets have also been a great test and a punishment for humanity. Each Prophet has come challenging the norms of the age in which he lived and humanity has brought upon itself afflictions and punishment for having rejected the Prophets.

Now, we will examine each one of the seven stages, in order to test this hypothesis and to determine which Prophet pertains to each successive stage.

REFERENCES

1. For a fuller explanation of this topic, the reader should refer to the book, *Some Answered Questions* by 'Abdu'l-Bahá.
2. Of the seven cities related to the seven Churches of Revelation, three of them (Smyrna, Pergamos, and Thyatira) still exist with the names of Izmir, Bergamo and Akhisar respectively. Ephesus was destroyed by the Goths in 262 D.C. and Sardis existed until the last years of the Byzantine Empire.

CHAPTER 4

Stages I to IV

The First Stage

The letter to the first church gives us a clear indication as to which Prophet this stage pertains. There is mention of a "fall" and of the "Tree of Life".

> "Remember therefore from whence thou art fallen, and repent, and do the first works" (Rev. 2:5)"
>
> "He that hath an ear, let him hear what the Spirit saith unto the churches; To him that overcometh will I give to eat of the tree of life, which is in the midst of the paradise of God." (Rev. 2:7)

The reference to a fall reminds us of the story of Adam, who fell from grace in the garden of Eden. With respect to the Tree of Life, in Genesis 2 we read:

> "And the Lord God planted a garden eastward in Eden; and there he put the man whom he had formed. And out of the ground made the Lord God to grow every tree that is pleasant to the sight; the tree of life also in the midst of the garden...." (Gen. 2:8-9)

The references in Revelation to a fall and to the Tree of Life, suggest a relationship between Adam and the first stage of Revelation: Adam is the first Prophet of Revelation.

What other relationship exists between Adam and the events of the first stage? With the first plague, there is mention of "men with the mark of the beast" (Rev. 16:2). This reminds us of the story of Cain, Adam's son, who killed his brother Abel (Gen. 4). For his crime Cain was marked by God. We read that the blood of Abel fell over the earth and God made the earth unproductive. Similarly, in Revelation, when the first trumpet sounds, it says that "there followed hail and fire mingled with blood, and they were cast upon the earth: and the third part of trees was burnt up, and all green grass was burnt up" (Rev. 8:7). As Cain and Abel lived in the epoch of Adam, their story forms part of the first of the seven stages of Revelation.

We should mention that the Biblical stories cited here possibly have symbolic meanings, but these we will not discuss here. Our purpose in this instance is to demonstrate similarities between Revelation and the other Biblical accounts cited, without interpreting these accounts in detail.

In relation to Genesis, the first day saw the creation of the first light. Adam, being the first Prophet, brought the first spiritual light to the world.

The Second Stage

We will recall that the second stage is marked by references to the SEA, BLOOD, and DEATH. What Prophet is linked to the SEA, and with death and destruction? The age of Noah is known as an age of general destruction. In reality, the flood is the greatest disaster that is mentioned in all the world's literature. Noah is the second Prophet of Revelation, in whose age DEATH came by means of the SEA.

The Third Stage

In the third stage there are various signs that clearly indicate that Moses is the Prophet of this age. For example, with the third plague, the rivers and fountains turn to BLOOD (Rev. 16:4). This is a reference to the second miracle that Moses performed before Pharaoh:

"...and he lifted up the rod and smote the waters that were in the river, in sight of Pharaoh, and in the sight of his servants; and all the waters that were in the river were turned into blood." (Exo. 7:20)

Also, upon opening the third seal, there appears "a black horse and he that sat on him had a pair of balances" (Rev. 6:5). The balance has always been a symbol of the law and of justice. Moses was the author of the Law.

In the letter to the third church, there is a warning to those who follow "the doctrine of Balaam, who taught Balak to cast a stumblingblock before the children of Israel" (Rev. 2:14).

This is a reference to the story of Balaam, a priest in the days of Moses (Num. 22).

In Genesis, the third day was that in which the earth was created. We read:

> "And God said, Let the waters under the heaven be gathered together unto one place, and let the dry land appear... And God called the dry land Earth." (Gen. 1:9)

This also reminds us of another miracle attributed to Moses, that of parting the Red Sea:

> "And Moses stretched out his hand over the sea; and the Lord caused the sea to go back by a strong east wind all that night, and made the sea dry land, and the waters were divided." (Exo. 14:21)

We see that the events of the third stage are related to the events of the Dispensation of Moses, which suggests that Moses is the third Prophet. We should repeat that these miracles of the Bible may have symbolic meanings which we can not explore in this study. Our purpose is to establish a parallel between Revelation and the previous accounts of the Biblical Prophets, in order to demonstrate that Revelation has a relationship with these stories.

The Fourth Stage

One expects that the stage of spiritual evolution that should follow that of Moses would be the Christian Dispensation, which would be the fourth stage of Revelation.

In the letter directed to the fourth church (Thyatira) the author of Revelation says:

"I know thy works, and charity, and service, and faith, and thy patience." (Rev. 2:19)

These virtues do not pertain exclusively to Christians, but they do have a special role in the Message of Jesus; for example, Paul emphasizes "faith, hope, and charity" (1 Cor. 13:13) as the three principle Christian virtues.

There is also a promise to Thyatira that it should have "power over the nations" (Rev. 2:26). These words remind us of another promise of Jesus: "And this gospel of the kingdom shall be preached in all the world, for a witness unto all nations" (Mat. 24:14).

It is well known among Christians that the Mission of Jesus was not exclusively for the Jews, but also for the Gentiles. To this Jesus refers in the Evangel saying that it would be preached to all nations. Christianity was the first of the religions to attain a world-wide projection, far beyond that of any previous religion. To this refers the promise in Revelation of a "power over the nations".

There is another reference to the world-wide extension and power of Christianity when the fourth seal is opened (Rev. 6:8). A pale horse appears with a rider whose name is death, who receives power "over the fourth part of the earth". Christianity has fulfilled this promise in so much as about one fourth of the world population is Christian. Numerically Christianity is the largest religion which exists and no other religion accounts for one fourth of the world population.

To some it may seem strange to think that the Cause of Christ is represented by a pale horse and a rider called "death", who comes to "kill with sword" (Rev. 6:8). The words of Jesus are the best testimony of this relationship when He says: "I came not to send peace, but a SWORD" (Mat. 10:34). For the Jews these words represented a severe chastisement: "And they shall fall by the edge of the sword" (Luke 21:24). And years later, (although contrary to the wishes of Jesus) the sword would be the principal means of propagating Christianity among the barbarians of Europe and to some degree, among the natives of the Americas and Africa.

We noted previously in the analysis of the fourth stage that there are various references to heavenly bodies: the sun, the moon and the stars. In the book of Acts, Peter quotes a prophecy of Joel to show the relationship between the Dispensation of Jesus and the signs in the sun and the moon:

> "But this is that which was spoken by the prophet Joel,... The sun shall be turned into darkness, and the moon into blood...."
> (Acts 2:16-20)

The mention which is made of the celestial bodies in the holy books is in reference rather to the heavenly beings: to God, to His Messengers and to the Apostles and clergy of each religion. In other cases the celestial bodies are in reference to the religion and its laws and teachings. In the Bible we find this use of symbols. For example: Jesus said, "I am the way, the truth, and the light" and in Psalms 84:11 we read, "For the Lord God is a sun and shield". To say that "the sun shall be turned into darkness" means that the previous religion will be a dark and dead thing, having lost its spiritual life. Such was the state of Judaism when Jesus came.

In another sense, Jesus himself came with the authority to "darken the sun", that is, to abrogate or modify the laws and practices of the Judaic religion. Revelation says:

"...and the third part of the sun was smitten, and the third part of the moon, and the third part of the stars..." (Rev. 8:12)

A possible interpretation of this passage is that Jesus eliminated a part of the Mosaic Law but confirmed another part leaving it unchanged. Later the Apostles made other modifications to the law.

In conclusion: The fourth stage of Revelation refers to the Dispensation of Jesus.

Chapter 5

The Remaining Three Stages

Continuing on to the fifth stage, we note that the accounts in Revelation are much more detailed. For example, the accounts of the first four trumpets occupy only six verses of Chapter 8. But the accounts of the other three trumpets occupy all of chapters 9, 10 and 11.

Why are the fifth, sixth, and seventh stages more detailed?

We remember that Revelation was written in the first years of the Christian era. We have shown that the first four stages represent four divine Dispensations that came to the world through Adam, Noah, Moses and Christ respectively. Then what do the fifth, sixth and seventh stages represent?

Just as the first four stages represent four divine revelations, so also do the last three. But the last three are stages to come and represent future revelations of future Prophets after Christ. This is the part of Revelation which is truly prophetic and for this reason is more detailed.

That Prophets are to come after Jesus is clear and explicit in the text of Revelation, and for those who doubt this, Chapter 11 offers sufficient

The Remaining Three Stages

testimony. In Revelation 11 we read of "two witnesses" who are "two prophets" and who have great powers to "shut heaven, that it rain not in the days of their prophecy: and have power over waters to turn them to blood" (Rev. 11:6). These were powers of Elias and Moses respectively[1]; thus we see that these two Prophets of Revelation are Prophets in every sense of the word.

It is thus evident that the prophetic line did not end with Jesus, or, in other words, that the process of spiritual evolution which we have called "progressive revelation" was destined to continue even after the Revelation that Jesus bestowed upon His followers.

These verses confirm that which our study of the seven stages implies, that after the Christian Dispensation (the fourth stage), new revelations are to come to the world in the future. Specifically, three stages of Revelation remain to be defined, each one of which must be initiated by a Prophet.

It is clear that, when Revelation was written, the future included all of the last 1,900 years. What has occurred in the spiritual evolution of man in these 1,900 years? We will interrupt our study of Revelation to answer this question, and to acquaint ourselves with the historical events, a knowledge of which is necessary to understand the fifth, sixth and seventh stages.

Muḥammad, Prophet of God

Muḥammad is the Prophet of the fifth stage and the founder of Islám. Although Muḥammad has been scorned in the West for many years, there are in fact many Biblical prophecies that testify to the truth of His Mission. For example, to the descendants of Ishmael, son of Abraham, the promise was given that they should be "a great nation" (Gen. 21:18).

The descendants of Ishmael are the Arabs and it was Muḥammad who established them as "a great nation".

In another Biblical passage we read:

"The Lord came from Sinai, and rose up from Seir unto them; he shined forth from mount Paran, and he came with ten thousands of saints..." (Deut. 33:2).

The coming of the Lord from Sinai is in reference to Moses, because there Moses received His Revelation. The Lord who came from Seir is in reference to Jesus; Seir is a mountain in Palestine. The Lord who shone forth from PARAN is in reference to Muḥammad. Paran is a chain of mountains in Arabia, native land of Muḥammad. Paran is mentioned specifically as the land of the descendants of Ishmael (Gen. 21:21), thus establishing a relationship between these mountains and the Arabs. The Lord who came with ten thousand saints refers to yet another Prophet of the two which we still have not identified.

Another prophecy about Mount Paran appears in the book of Habakkuk:

"God came from Teman, and the Holy One from mount Paran." (Hab. 3:3)

This prophecy says clearly that a Saint (Prophet) is to come from Mount Paran and from

The Remaining Three Stages

Teman, which is an ancient name for Arabia. It is said that many Jews that lived in Arabia in the time of Muḥammad, accepted Him as a Prophet because they saw in Him the fulfillment of this prophecy[2].

These references of the Old Testament are quoted here as additional evidence of the Divine Mission of Muḥammad, but the allusions to Muḥammad abound in the book of Revelation also, as we will soon see. To understand these references, we will need to make a brief summary of the history of Muḥammad and His religion.

Muḥammad was born in Arabia in the city of Mecca in the VI century of the Christian Era, in a family that earned their living attending the pilgrims who arrived to visit sites of worship there. Although the Arabs traced their descendance from Abraham and worshiped in the Kaaba (temple supposedly built by Abraham Himself), by the time of Muḥammad they had fallen into the pagan practice of honoring a multitude of gods whose graven images encircled the Kaaba. Having been isolated from the line of the Hebrew Prophets, they recognized neither Moses nor Jesus. Socially, the Arabs lived in tribes of extended families that were in a constant state of war.

Muḥammad worked as a merchant and was known for His rectitude and piety. At times He retired to the mountains to pray and meditate, and on one of these occasions God spoke to Him, raising Him to the station of Prophethood.

The Arabs rejected Muḥammad violently when He challenged their traditional beliefs, denying the pagan gods, and insisting on the oneness of the one true God and reverence for Moses, Jesus and the other Israelite Prophets. Muḥammad suffered insults and persecution for thirteen years and during this period His most faithful followers were Alí, His cousin, and Khadijih, His wife. Finally Muḥammad abandoned Mecca, relocating to the north in the city of Medina, where the majority of the inhabitants accepted Him and received Him as their King and Governor. Muḥammad's migration from Mecca to Medina in 622 A.D. is known as the Hegira and marks the beginning of the Moslem calendar which is governed by the lunar year. The Hegira was the beginning of the triumph of Muḥammad; within a few years He had united the warring tribes of Arabia in one common Cause, whose unifying force was the new Faith. Even the enemies of Muḥammad have testified to His great administrative ability in fusing the Arabs in one single nation.

Once established in Medina, Muḥammad waged military campaigns against those who opposed Him. These military campaigns have been the object of criticism on the part of observers of Islám in the West, but several points must be made in defense of Muḥammad.

1. The campaigns of Muḥammad were, for the most part, defensive. His enemies ferociously attacked Him and His followers and left them no recourse but to defend themselves.

2. When Muḥammad was alone and suffered the calumnies and threats of the people of Mecca, He did not resort to self-defense, but exposed Himself to the attacks of the Arabs. Later, when He migrated to Medina and the people there accepted Him as their King, Muḥammad responded not only for His own well being, but for the well being and security of His people, including women and children. More than a spiritual leader, Muḥammad was also a ruler and head of state, and in that capacity. He was obliged to protect His people. In this sense, He was no different than Moses.
3. All of the Prophets of God have exercised judgement over those who have opposed them. Some in the West have critized Muḥammad, comparing Him with Jesus who gave His life with meekness. However, they forget that Jesus also judged the Jews who rejected Him: "... they shall fall by the edge of the sword, and shall be led away captive into all nations..." (Luke 21:24). The judgement which Muḥammad exercised over the Arabs for some ten years was in no way more severe than the punishment which the Jews suffered for nineteen centuries.

Muḥammad taught principles which agree with those of Christianity, including reverence toward Jesus, Moses, and the other Prophets; submission before the one true God; the future Day of Judgement; and reward and punishment in a life after death.

On various occasions, Muḥammad had expressed His desire that Alí should be His successor and when He found Himself on His deathbed, He requested a secretary to dictate a testament naming Alí as leader of the Islamic Faith after Himself. But certain persons would not permit this, and thus Muḥammad died without establishing an authority after Him. This was fatal for the future of Islám, because old jealousies quickly resurged and the Moslems warred for many years over the question of succession. As a result two parallel lines of succession arose after Muḥammad, one legitimate and one illegitimate. The legitimate line began with Alí and continued with eleven other successors; these twelve successors are the Imáms of Shi'ah Islám. This line lasted 260 lunar years, after which the 12th Imám disappeared, a boy of only 5 years of age. There are various versions of the story, but the Shi'ah orthodox believe that the last Imám remained hidden for several years, communicating with the world by means of four successive spokesmen. When the fourth spokesman died, all contact with the Hidden Imám was lost, but the Shi'ahs believe that this Imám still lives and will return on the Day of Judgement to establish justice and the reign of peace in the world.

The illegitimate line of successors to Muḥammad consisted in a series of dynasties that took power by force: first the Ummayyad, later the 'Abbasid, and more recently, the Caliphs of the Turkish Ottomans. These dynasties always bore enmity for the Imáms and assassinated several of them. Especially moving was the case of Husayn, grandson of Muhammad and third Imám, who died on the plain of Karbilá in Mesopotamia together with seventy of his companions. Husayn and his companions were surrounded and dying of thirst, when the Ummayad army of four thousand men confronted them and massacred them mercilessly.

Husayn is one of the most heroic figures in all the history of religion, known not only for his courage but for his generosity and spirituality. After having seen his friends fall in battle, and having suffered the death of his infant son by an enemy arrow while he carried him in his arms, Husayn still held no rancor for his persecutors. Until his last breath, instead of imploring mercy for himself, he begged his enemies to repent and cease the slaughter for their own sakes. We only find a comparable example of forgiveness in the martyrdom of Jesus Himself.

The assassins of Husayn, not satisfied with his death, trampled his body with horses and decapitated him, carrying his head on the point of a lance from city to city and celebrating his death for days. Such that the eminent Western historian, Gibbon, wrote, "In a distant age and clime, the tragic scene of the death of Husayn will awaken the compassion of the coldest reader"[3].

Until this day enmity exists between Shi'ah Moslems (followers of the Imáms) and Sunni

Moslems (followers of the Caliphs). The Shi'ahs are concentrated in Irán, Iráq and Lebanon, while the Sunni are mostly in Turkey, Arabia and other Islamic countries.

The internal strife of Islám destroyed forever the unity of the Moslems; but it could not prevent that, over the years, the impulse given to history by Muḥammad should yield its fruits. The Islamic civilization born of the Message of Muḥammad was, from the eighth until the fifteenth century, the most advanced upon the face of the earth. While the Europeans were submerged in the darkness of the Middle Ages, the Arabs dedicated themselves to the study of medicine, astronomy, mathematics, architecture, and agriculture, stimulated by the command of the Prophet to seek knowledge "even unto China". The erudite Moslems studied the writings of the ancient Greeks, Egyptians, Persians and Hindus and filled great libraries with their books and with original works. They established universities of renown, such as the Al-Azhar in Cairo, which at present is the oldest functioning institution of higher learning in the world. Many European nobles sent their sons to study in these centers of knowledge, particularly in Spain. In one unusual case cited by the North American historian, Draper, one of those Europeans named Gerbert returned to his native country and years later became the Supreme Pontiff of the Catholic Church, Pope Silvester II[4].

We all recognize the contribution of the Arabs to mathematics in what we call Arabic

The Remaining Three Stages

numbers, borrowed from the Hindus and transmitted to Europe and to posterity. The Arabic numbers and the decimal system were a prerequisite for the rebirth of European science under Galileo, Copernicus and others. The Arabs inherited the compass from the Chinese and with this they made advances in the science of navigation. The Portuguese learned navigation from the Arabs, and Cristopher Colombus, in turn, from the Portuguese. Thus the Arabs contributed tangibly to the opening of the so-called New World. To them we owe an impressive list of things transmitted from other cultures or invented by themselves, such as, the windmill; industrial acids; soap; distilled alcohol; algebra; paper; textiles such as silk; crops such as cotton, rice, sugar cane, and coffee; fruits like cherries, apricots, peaches, apples, oranges and dates; tulips; and even the guitar[5]. Many of these contributions entered our Western culture through Spain, and others through Sicily.

However, many historians agree that the greatest contribution of Muḥammad was in the field of political science and in the construction of nations. From the outset, love of one's country was an element of Islám which never existed in any previous religion. It is said that Muḥammad himself produced the first written constitution, that of Medina, in which were defined the rights of citizens and the duties of the rulers[6]. That which Moses did for the Israelite tribes by revealing the Law, Muḥammad did for the nations, promoting principles of social justice and creating a spirit of national citizenship which never existed before.

Such a summary of Islamic civilization is necessarily brief, but essential if we are to judge the Prophet of Islám by the criterion of Jesus: "by their fruits ye shall know them"; and if we are to appreciate the scope of the prophecy, given to Ishmael and His descendants: "I will make of him a Great Nation" (Gen. 21:18). Undoubtedly, future authors will explore more deeply the relationship between the sister civilizations of Christianity and Islám. To them we leave this task and return to the theme of the Prophets of Revelation.

The Báb, the Promised One of Islám

The Shi'ah Moslems await a Promised One called the Qá'im, who will come according to them, in miraculous circumstances to establish His kingdom in all the world. In the last century, two Moslem saints, Shaykh Ahmad and Siyyid Kázim, arose successively to announce to the Shi'ahs that the advent of the Promised One was near, declaring that the signs of His coming mentioned in the Islamic traditions had a symbolic significance.

In the year 1844 A.D. in Shiráz, Persia, a Youth of twenty-five years of age, Siyyid 'Alí Muhammad, announced that He was this Promised One. The year 1844 A.D. corresponds with the year 1260 of the Moslem calendar, that is, exactly one thousand lunar years after the line of the twelve Shi'ah Imáms disappeared.

The Remaining Three Stages

Siyyid 'Alí Muḥammad took the title of the Báb, which means "The Gate". The Báb gathered around Himself eighteen disciples called the Letters of the Living, the last of these being Quddús, a twenty-one year old youth, who with only seeing Him walk and observing the perfection of His gait, accepted the Báb as the promised Qá'im. Quddús occupied an outstanding position among the disciples of the Báb, comparable with Peter among the Apostles of Christ.

The Báb dispatched the Letters of the Living to spread the new Message, with the exception of Quddús, whom He took with Him on pilgrimage to the holy cities of Mecca and Medina in Arabia. There the Báb declared His Message to the Moslem world, but the Sherif of Mecca, custodian of the holy places, received the announcement with indifference and lost the opportunity to investigate the Báb's claims.

Upon His return to Persia, the Báb found that the opposition to the new Message was already growing. Just as the Pharisees conspired against Jesus, the Moslem priests were the principal opponents of the Báb. They incited the rulers to imprison the Báb and outlaw the teaching of His Message. However, the Bábi Faith grew rapidly among all social classes, attracting some of the most renowned Moslem clergy of the time as well.

Such was the impact of the Báb upon the Persian society that its drama attracted the attention of many European writers. A theatrical performance based on His life was presented in Saint Peterburg, Russia and the French historian, Ernest Renan, commented: "Bábism...in Persia has been an extraordinary phenomenon. A sweet and non-pretentious man...modest and pious, I have seen, almost against His will, raised to a station of prophet, of incarnated divinity and came to be the ardent and fervent head of a creed named after him"[7].

The king of Persia, Muḥammad Shah, apparently had a sincere desire to meet the Báb and investigate His cause, since he gave an order to call Him to his capital, Tehrán, for an interview. But his prime minister, a man jealous of his position and afraid of losing his influence with the king, intervened to "postpone" the interview. When the Báb was nearing Tehrán, a counter-order was issued and the Báb was conducted under guard to an ancient castle in Mah-Ku, Adhir'bayjan, a remote province of Persia and far from population centers. Thus, the prime minister and the priests hoped to isolate the Báb and minimize His influence, but even there the local populace felt irresistibly attracted to the Báb and His fame spread ever wider.

In the meantime, the Bábis (followers of the Báb) were attacked by army troops and had to take refuge in improvised forts on several occasions. In the case of the battle of Fort Tabarsi, the Bábis defended themselves against the onslaught of the soldiers of the royal army for several months. Ready to die for their new Faith, the Bábis could only be conquered when

The Remaining Three Stages

their attackers swore on the Qurán that they would let them leave in safety. Once outside of the fort, the army attacked and annihilated the majority of them.

The earthly Mission of the Báb was now coming to its end when He was moved again from Mah'Ku to the castle of Chihriq and imprisoned there. At that time the priests convened a council to interrogate Him in the city of Tabríz. The council was attended by the Prince and future King of Persia, Nasir, and a number of hostile priests whose intentions were to discredit the Báb. In a scene reminiscent of the interrogation of Jesus before Annas and Caiphas, the Báb was humiliated by the priests with insults. But the Báb responded with complete confidence and declared:

"I am, I am, I am, the Promised One! I am the One whose name you have for a thousand years invoked, at whose mention you have risen, whose advent you have longed to witness, and the hour of whose Revelation you have prayed God to Hasten. Verily I say, it is incumbent upon the peoples of both the East and the West to obey My word and to pledge allegiance to My person."[8]

The interrogation ended when the Báb strode out of the meeting of His own accord. But confronted with the declaration which He had made before his enemies, the decision of the priests was the same as that of Annas and

Caiphas with regards to Jesus: The Báb must die. On the 9th of July, 1850, the Báb was suspended against a wall in the public square of Tabríz, together with a young follower who begged for the honor of dying with his Master. The Báb directed his last words to the multitude of some ten thousand persons who had congregated to see the spectacle:

"Had you believed in Me, O wayward generation, every one of you would have followed the example of this youth, who stood in rank above most of you, and willingly would have sacrificed himself in My path. The day will come when you will have recognized Me; that day I shall have ceased to be with you."[9]

Thereafter a regiment of seven hundred fifty soldiers aimed their rifles at the breast of the Báb and in an instant the bullets took the precious life of yet another of the Messengers of God. So has it come to pass since the beginning of the history of mankind.

The remains of the Báb were rescued and held in hiding for nearly fifty years, until the day they were moved to Mount Carmel in Israel where today they rest in a beautiful sanctuary that adorns the Holy Mountain of God.

Throughout His brief but tempestuous earthly Mission, the Báb announced to His followers that the day of the Revelation of still another Prophet, the One whose appearance He had come to announce, was near. Thus, just as John the Baptist prepared the way for Jesus, the Báb was preparing the hearts to receive "Him whom God shall make manifest". After the martyrdom of the Báb, the hopes of the Bábis were set upon that promise, repeated many times in His Writings in which He had declared: "Of all the tributes I have paid to Him Who is to come after Me the greatest is this, my written confession that no words of Mine can adequately describe Him, nor can any reference to Him in My Book, the Bayan, do justice to His Cause."[10]

"The germ that holds within itself the potentialities of the Revelation that is to come is endowed with a potency superior to the combined forces of all those who follow me."[11]

Bahá'u'lláh—The Glory of God

In the first days of the Dispensation of the Báb, one who spontaneously accepted His Message by only reading His Writings was Mírzá Husayn 'Alí, a member of one of the most outstanding families of Tehrán and a descendant of the ancient Sasanian kings of Persia. The father of Mírzá Husayn 'Alí had been a respected minister in the court of the Shah, position which, upon his death was offered to his son. However, Mirzá Husayn 'Alí refused the offer (something most unusual in that world of intrigues of the royal court) and dedicated Himself to His "profession". One of His contemporaries said that His occupation was "to cheer the disconsolate and feed the hungry", that of rank and position He had none "apart from befriending the poor and the stranger."[12]

Upon accepting the Message of the Báb, Mírzá Husayn 'Alí became one of the most fervent followers of the new Faith, teaching the Message widely, attracting many people to the new Revelation and debating difficult points of Islamic doctrine upon which He had had no formal training, with the erudite priests. In this period He became known as Bahá'u'lláh, a title by which the Báb Himself referred to Him and which means the Glory of God.

In 1853, three years after the martyrdom of the Báb and in the midst of a wave of persecution which took the lives of some 20,000 Bábis, Bahá'u'lláh was made prisoner and chained in the Black Pit, a horrible subterranean prison where neither light nor fresh air entered. Upon His neck were placed chains and fetters that weighed over one hundred pounds; His companions, except for some 40 Bábis, were thieves and assassins. In this dark place God revealed to Bahá'u'lláh that He was the One whose coming the Báb had prepared.

Bahá'u'lláh has left this description of His divine experience in that Black Pit:

> "One night in a dream, these exalted words were heard on every side: 'Verily, We shall render Thee victorious by Thyself and by Thy pen. Grieve Thou not for that which hath befallen

The Remaining Three Stages

Thee, neither be Thou afraid, for Thou art in safety. Ere long will God raise up the treasures of the earth—men who will aid Thee through Thyself and through Thy Name, wherewith God hath revived the hearts of such as have recognized Him."

Bahá'u'lláh is the seventh Prophet of Revelation.

After four months in the prison, Bahá'u'lláh was freed, but with the condition that He leave Persia forever. In the midst of bitter cold and a terrible snow storm, Bahá'u'lláh and His family crossed the mountains of Western Persia en route to Baghdád, thus beginning banishments which lasted forty years, and which only ended with His death.

Bahá'u'lláh lived ten years in Baghdád, the city on the banks of the Tigris that had served in the past as seat of the Abbasid Caliphate. Over the centuries, Baghdád had lost its former glory, but was still a provincial capital of the Turkish Empire. It was situated near the holy places of the Shi'ah sect: the tombs of the Imáms Alí and Husayn, and the cities of Karbila, Kázimayn and Najaf which were centers of Shi'ah theology. Therefore, many Moslem pilgrims and religious leaders passed through Baghdád on their way to these places and so were exposed to the wisdom of Bahá'u'lláh. Such was the respect which the people held for Him, that the Moslem clergy grew jealous, concerned for their own position and influence.

They conspired against Bahá'u'lláh and convinced the government of Turkey to move Him to Constantinople, seat of the Turkish Empire and far from Baghdád. But this would not be the last of His Banishments.

In all, Bahá'u'lláh suffered four banishments which took Him finally to the penal colony of 'Akká on the coast of Palestine.[14] In that time 'Akká was a remote corner of the Turkish Empire, a prison where political prisoners and the worst of criminals were sent. Bahá'u'lláh, His family, and small number of His followers arrived in 'Akká in August of 1868, and here the tribulations of Bahá'u'lláh reached their climax. So pestilent was the city that the daughter of Bahá'u'lláh, already accustomed to severe hardship, could not withstand the onerous smell and fainted. Weakened by malnutrition and dysentery, some of the Bahá'ís died in the first months. But the climax came when the youngest son of Bahá'u'lláh, Mírzá Mihdí, suffered injuries that caused his death. Mírzá Mihdí was known as the Most Pure Branch and was the incarnation of piety and humility. He had gone up to the roof of the prison to pray, and as he paced, concentrated in his devotions, he fell through a skylight. His last wish before dying twenty-two hours later, was that God would permit that the prison doors be opened to the visits of the Bahá'ís. The death of Mírzá Mihdí was an incalculable loss for Bahá'u'lláh.

Bahá'u'lláh spent a total of two years, two months, and five days in the prison and another

The Remaining Three Stages

seven years within the city, restricted to a house where His only exercise was to pace about His room. After the passing of nine years, Bahá'u'lláh had gained the respect and love of the authorities and clergy of 'Akká, who insisted that He leave the city and live in the countryside.

There Bahá'u'lláh spent the last twelve years of His life in peace and tranquility. It was during this period that He visited Mount Carmel, Holy Mountain of the Bible, some twenty kilometers from the city of 'Akká on the other side of the Bay of Haifa. It was also in this period, in the year 1890, that a distinguished professor of the University of Cambridge, England, Doctor Edward Granville Browne, came to Palestine for the purpose of visiting Bahá'u'lláh. He has left the following description of the first of four interviews with Bahá'u'lláh, which is the only existing account by a European of his impressions in His presence.

"The face of Him on Whom I gazed I can never forget, though I cannot describe it. Those piercing eyes seemed to read one's very soul; power and authority sat on that ample brow; while the deep lines on the forehead and face implied an age which the jet black hair and beard flowing down in indistinguishable luxuriance almost to the waist seemed to belie. No need to ask in Whose presence I stood, as I bowed myself before One Who is the object of a devotion and love which kings might envy and emperors sigh for in vain!

A mild dignified voice bade me be seated, and then continued: "Praise be to God that thou has attained! ... Thou hast come to see a prisoner and an exile..... We desire but the good of the world and the happiness of the nations; yet they deem us a stirrer-up of strife and sedition worthy of bondage and banishment..... That all nations should become one in faith, and all men as brothers; that the bonds of affection and unity between the sons of men should be strengthened; that diversity of religion should cease, and differences of race be annulled—what harm is there in this? .... Yet so it shall be; these fruitless strifes, these ruinous wars shall pass away, and the Most Great Peace shall come..... Is this not that which Christ foretold? .... These strifes and this bloodshed and discord must cease, and all men be as one kindred and one family."[15]

During the forty years of His Mission, Bahá'u'lláh revealed a collection of religious literature without equal in the history of religion: more than one hundred volumes of prayers and meditations, laws and ordinances, social teachings, and commentaries on holy books of the Jews, Christians, and Moslems. A great part

The Remaining Three Stages

of this spiritual wealth was written by Bahá'u'lláh in His own hand and the remainder was dictated to secretaries and reviewed by Him personally, in such manner that the authenticity of the Bahá'í Writings is indisputable.

The principles propagated by the Bahá'í Faith have the objective of educating humanity and preparing it for the unification of humankind. Bahá'u'lláh taught precepts such as: equality between men and women; elimination of all types of prejudice whether it be racial, religious, national, or of social class; universal education; world peace which will be established by a universal council; essential harmony between science and religion; the essential oneness of all the great religions of the world. These and other precepts are the foundation of the Bahá'í Faith.

Bahá'u'lláh died on May 29, 1892, in the mansion of Bahjí, four kilometers from 'Akká, His sanctuary, the Most Sacred Spot for the Bahá'ís of the world, is found there.

Bahá'u'lláh left a written Testament or Covenant, in which He named his eldest son, 'Abdu'l-Bahá, as His successor and as central authority of the Bahá'í Faith after Him. We can appreciate the transcendental significance of the Covenant of Bahá'u'lláh if we consider for a moment the divisions which have splintered the religions of the past for the lack of a similar document. The disagreements between Protestants and Catholics, between Sunnis and Shi'ahs, are basically disagreements over the succession of authority after the Founder of the respective religion. In the cases of Christianity and Islám, these disagreements have resulted in bloodshed for centuries, a situation which persists until today. The Covenant of Bahá'u'lláh assures that the Bahá'í Faith will not suffer such divisions.

'Abdu'l-Bahá directed the fortunes of the Bahá'í Faith for twenty-nine years and during the period of His Ministry the Faith extended to Europe and North America, to which He Himself travelled. Furthermore, 'Abdu'l-Bahá supervised the construction of the Sanctuary of the Báb upon Mount Carmel and personally deposited the remains of the Báb in their place. He was loved by all the residents of Haifa where He passed His last years. The government of Great Britain even recognized His works of charity and service to the people of Palestine during the First World War, and designated Him a knight of the United Kingdom.

When 'Abdu'l-Bahá died in 1921, He left a Testament of His own in which He named His grandson, Shoghi Effendi, to be the Guardian of the Faith. The Testament of 'Abdu'l-Bahá is an extension on the Covenant of Bahá'u'lláh and maintains the succession of authority which Bahá'u'lláh established. Shoghi Effendi administered the Bahá'í Faith for thirty-six years, during which he prepared the Bahá'í world for the election of the Universal House of Justice, supreme body established in the Writings of Bahá'u'lláh as the unique legislative body of the Faith. The House of Justice is authorized to create new laws, according to future needs, thus assuring the flexibility to meet the demands of a rapidly changing world.

Shoghi Effendi died in 1957, but a group of his principal aids, designated as Hands of the Cause of God, assured the completion of his plan. In 1963 the Universal House of Justice was elected by representatives of the Bahá'ís throughout the world, thus maintaining the succession of the authority established by Bahá'u'lláh in His Covenant. The Seat of the Universal House of Justice is found on the slopes of Mount Carmel and is the World Center of this New Faith.

The reader should consult the Bahá'í literature for more information about the lives of the Báb and Bahá'u'lláh and the history of the Bahá'í Faith. For our purpose, the information presented is sufficient to proceed with the study of the seven stages of Revelation.

REFERENCES

1. See 1st Kings 17:1 and Exo. 7:17.
2. Elena Maria Marsella, *The Quest for Eden*, p. 199.
3. Edward Gibbon, *The Decline and Fall of the Roman Empire*, quoted in *The Spirit of Islám*, by Syed Ameer Alí, p. 302.
4. John William Draper, *The Intellectual Development of Europe*, quoted in *The Secret of Divine Civilization*, by 'Abdu'l-Bahá pp. 92-93.
5. Stanwood Cobb, *Islamic Contributions to Civilization*, pp. 47-60.
6. M. Hamidullah, *Introduction to Islám*, pp. 11-12.
7. Ernest Renan, *Les Apotres*, quoted in *Rumbo Hacia el Futuro* by Gayle Wooleson, p. 42.

8. Shoghi Effendi, *Dawnbreakers*, pp. 159-160.
9. Ibid, p. 192.
10. Shoghi Effendi, *The Dispensation of Bahá'u'lláh*, p. 8.
11. Ibid, p. 8.
12. Shoghi Effendi, *Dawnbreakers*, pp. 105-106.
13. Shoghi Effendi, *God Passes By*, p. 101.
14. Akká has a long history that begins centuries before Christ. At one time it was an important Roman port and in the Middle Ages was the seat of a Christian kingdom during the Crusades. The wall that surrounds the city was built by the Turks and this successfully defied Napoleon's cannons. The Turks used the fort as a prison in the days of Bahá'u'lláh, and even during the English occupation of Palestine in this century, rebellious Jewish nationalists were imprisoned there. Akká is identified with Achor in the Bible where it is called "a door of hope" in the last days (Hosca 2:15).
15. Edward Granville Browne, Introduction to *A Traveller's Narrative,* quoted in *Bahá'u'lláh and the New Era*, by John Esslemont p. 39.

CHAPTER 6

Chapter 11 of Revelation: The Two Witnesses

We mentioned before that chapter 11 is dedicated to "two witnesses" that are "two prophets". 'Abdu'l-Bahá offers us a novel explanation of this chapter that will help us to understand many symbols of Revelation. For a complete explanation, the reader should refer to "Some Answered Questions", chapter 11. We present here a summary of this explanation.

The two witnesses represent Muḥammad and His first disciple, 'Alí. The two brought a message from God to the Arabs, who violently rejected them both. The Revelation of Muḥammad was a divine discipline and a "torment" for the Arabs.

The Dispensation of Muḥammad lasted 1,260 lunar years, according to the Moslem calendar, until the coming of the Báb in 1844 A.D. (see Figure 1). There is reference to this period of 1,260 years in several verses of Revelation. First, we should clarify that in Biblical prophecies, one day signifies one year. This convention is widely accepted by students of Biblical prophecy, as is stated in Ezekiel 4:6,

"I have appointed thee each day for a year".

Thus we will see that the 1,260 lunar years of the Dispensation of Muḥammad are represented as:

1,260 days
42 months   (42 months x 30 days/month = 1,260 days = 1,260 years)
3½ years   (3½ years = 42 months = 1,260 days = 1,260 years)
3½ days   (3½ days = 3½ years = 1,260 days = 1,260 years)

In Revelation 11:3 we read, "...I will give unto my two witnesses, and they shall prophesy one thousand two hundred and three score days...." This is a reference to the duration of the Dispensation of Muḥammad, 1,260 days (1,260 years) in which the Revelation (testimony) of Muḥammad would have effected. But we remember that in the history of the religion of Muḥammad, there were always two lines of authority, one legitimate and the other illegitimate. It was not only the Dispensation of Muḥammad that lasted 1,260 years, but also the authority of His legitimate successors, and ALSO that of His illegitimate successors who opposed Him before and after His death. Later we will find further reference to the duration of that illegitimate authority.

"And when they shall have finished their testimony, the beast that ascendeth out of the bottomless pit shall make war against them and shall overcome them, and kill them." (Ref. 11:7)

Chapter 11 of Revelation : The Two Witnesses

This is a reference to the dynasties that opposed Muḥammad and usurped power after His death. The beast represents first the dynasty of the Umayyad, which had its center in Damascus, Syria.

> "And their dead bodies shall lie in the street of the great city, which spiritually is called Sodom and Egypt, where also our Lord was crucified." (Ref. 11:8)

This means that the opposers will conquer the forces of religion and the religion will be as a dead body. The reference to the great city where Jesus was crucified draws our attention to the region of Palestine and Syria, where the Umayyads had their capital in Damascus.

> "And they of the people and kindreds and tongues and nations shall see their dead bodies three days and a half..." (Rev. 11:9)

This is the period during which the religion will lie as a corpse, subjected to the illegitimate authority of the enemies of Muḥammad. We have already seen that 3½ days translates into 3½ years, or 1,260 days, or 1,260 years.

> "And after three days and an half, the spirit of life from God entered into them, and they stood upon their feet;..." (Rev. 11:11)

After 3½ days (1,260 years) the corpses, which is to say, the religion, will be renewed by the Spirit of God and the two Prophets will be resurrected. The period of 1,260 lunar years was fulfilled in 1844 A.D., the year that the Báb appeared. The two Prophets which will arise are the Báb and His foremost disciple, Quddus. Both the Báb and Quddus suffered martyrdom:

"And they ascended up to heaven in a cloud" (Rev. 11:12)

"In the same hour was there a great earthquake" (Rev. 11:13)

After the martyrdom of the Báb in Tabríz, Persia, at the other extreme of the country a terrible earthquake took place in shiráz, native city of the Báb, whose populace rejected, persecuted, and humiliated Him.

FIGURE 1
Correspondence between the Moslem and Gregorian Calendars of Some Dates Given in Revelation
Lunar Year of Moslem Calendar (AH)

1	260	856	1,260
622	874	1,453	1,844

Solar Year of Gregorian Calendar (AD)

622 AD=1AH	874 AD=260AH	1,453 AD=856AH	1,844 AD=1,260AH
*Muḥammad emigrates to Mecca from Medina. His migration is known as the hejira and begins the Moslem Calendar.	*The twelfth Imám of the Shi'ah Moslems disappears.	*Constantinople, seat of the Orthodox Church, falls to the Turks and later becomes the capital of the Ottoman Caliphs. *The 391 years spoken of in Rev. 9:15 begin.	*The Báb begins His Mission in Persia *1,260 lunar years of the Moslem Calendar end. *End of the 391 solar years mentioned in Rev. 9:15. *End of thousand lunar years since the disappearance of the last Shi'ah Imám.

All of the account of chapter 11 that we have discussed appears in the period of the sixth angel, but represents a bridge between the fifth and sixth stages. In the study of chapter 11 we have found important keys for understanding

Chapter 11 of Revelation : The Two Witnesses

these two stages: the meaning of the number 1,260, and the mysterious beast that comes from the pit, and its role in the history of religion. In future chapters we will see that this interpretation explains very well the historical events related to the period of Muḥammad. Now we will return to the fifth stage, to see how these keys serve us.

CHAPTER 7

The Fifth Stage

We have already indicated that Muḥammad is the Prophet of the fifth stage and we offer more evidence of this in other chapters. Here in Chapter Seven we will refer only to the events of the fifth stage which appear in Table 1 (Chapter 2) and which, in themselves, contain few details.

We noted already that in the letter to the fifth church, Sardis, there is mention of white robes for the saints. When the fifth seal of the book is opened (Rev. 6:9), the saints are identified as martyrs "slain for the word of God". Each religion has had its martyrs and the Bible relates the story of Stephen, first martyr (after Jesus) of the Christian church. Other martyrs fell in the persecution of the church by the Roman Empire. However, with the exception of the martyrdom of Christ Himself, the martyrs never played such a prominent role in the formation, beliefs, and attitudes of Christianity as they did in Islám. Even in the military campaigns which Muḥammad carried out, those who fell in battle as sacrifices for the Cause of God were considered as martyrs. Later, when the Umayyad

The Fifth Stage

persecuted the successors of Muḥammad, it was Ḥusayn, the grandson of Muḥammad, who was martyred together with his family and companions on the plain of Karbila, Iráq. Until this day the Shi'ah Moslems spend one month each year in mourning the tragic destiny of Ḥusayn.

Therefore, we suggest that the martyrs mentioned in the fifth stage of Revelation are the Moslem martyrs of the Cause of Muḥammad. We will refer again to these martyrs when we come to the sixth stage, and in the discussion of chapters 13 to 20 where we will find firmer evidence that these martyrs pertain to Islám.

In chapter 9, the trumpet of the fifth angel sounds and a star falls from heaven. This star was Abu-Sufyan, first of the line of the Ummayad, who opened the "bottomless pit", thus loosing the forces of opposition against Muḥammad. These are the same forces that came up from the bottomless pit in Chapter 11 and overcame the two Prophets (Muḥammad and Alí).

"And the sun and the air were darkened by reason of the smoke of the pit."

That is to say, the sun of the religion of Muḥammad was hidden by these forces of opposition.

"And to them it was given that they should not kill them, but that they should be tormented five months" (Rev. 9:5)

We have already seen that a day is one year in Biblical prophecy, therefore five months represent 150 days or 150 years. The Moslem conquerers, new power of the Middle East in the VII and VIII centuries, carried on a campaign of conquest that lasted about one hundred fifty years and expanded the Islamic Empire from Arabia to Persia and Spain.

We read that this destructive army only attacked the men "which have not the seal of God in their foreheads" (Rev. 9:4). The seal of God surely has a spiritual significance and represents a spiritual distinction among those that accepted the new Message, just as Paul told the first Christians that they were "sealed unto the day of redemption" with the "Holy Spirit of God" (Ephesians 4:30). The protection of the seal in Revelation is not security against corporal death, but against spiritual death, which is ignorance and unbelief.

However, in the case of the Moslems, "the seal of God in their foreheads" seems to have a literal fulfillment, insomuch as devout Moslems have the custom of praying five times daily and each time they prostrate themselves several times with the forehead to the ground. Over the years, this practice produces a slight discoloration or scar on the forehead that is a mark of the faith of the Moslem, a visible distinguishing "seal".

As we have seen, Chapter 11 speaks of Muḥammad and we have established a relationship between the Islamic history and references to the beast from the bottomless pit and the number 1,260. Later we will study other

The Fifth Stage

references to these signs, in order to see how these are related to the history of Muḥammad. But first we should complete the study of the seven stages as defined in Chapter 2.

CHAPTER 8

The Sixth Stage

We have said that the *sixth* stage pertains to the Báb and the *Seventh* to Bahá'u'lláh. These are the twin Prophets of the Bahá'í Faith and their names mean "The Gate" and "The Glory of God", respectively. We have explained that the Báb came as Precurser and that Bahá'u'lláh received His own Revelation shortly after the martyrdom of the Báb.

Upon reading the letter to the sixth church, we find: "I have set before thee an open door..." (Rev. 3:8) This door has a divine power, because "no man can shut" the door. Although Jesus also is identified as a door (John 10:9), in this case the door is the Báb, whose name means the Gate.

Here in the sixth latter there is also a promise of the return of the Jews to the Holy Land, which was one of the signs of the time of the end. It says "I will make them (the Jews) to come and worship before thy feet" (Rev. 3:9). How have these words been fulfilled?

The return of the Jews began in 1844 (year in which the Báb declared His mission) when the Sultan of Turkey signed the Edict of Toleration

The Six Stage

establishing religious freedom in all of the Turkish Empire, which included Palestine at that time. As a result of this Edict, the Jews began their modern exodus, which in time brought about a new Jewish nation.

Today the remains of the Báb rest in a beautiful Sanctuary on Mount Carmel in the Holy Land. Around His Sanctuary has grown the nation of Israel, inhabited by the Jews who worship God at the feet of the Báb, still unconscious of the divine power that has brought them back again to their promised land: "I will make them to come and worship before thy feet".

We have explained that the Mission of Bahá'u'lláh began only a few years after the Báb was martyred. We find reference to the rapid succession of their Missions in Revelation. Again in the letter to the sixth church, we read: "Behold, I come quickly" (Rev. 3:11). For centuries, Bible students have explained this verse saying that "quickly" for God may be a very long time for mankind, since "one day of the Lord is a thousand years". However, the warning "to come soon" has even more significance if we consider that it is directed to the followers of the Báb (the people of the sixth stage) warning them of the rapid advent of Bahá'u'lláh, who received His Revelation only three years after the martyrdom of the Báb.

There are other references in Revelation to the rapid succession of the sixth and seventh stages. In chapters 8 to 11, the seven angels sound their trumpets, and each of the last three angels are related with a "Woe". The fifth angel is the first "WOE"; the sixth angel is the second "WOE"; and the seventh angel is the third "WOE". At the end of the stage of the *sixth* angel we read:

"The second woe is past; and behold,
the third woe cometh quickly" (Rev. 11:14)

Here also reference is made to the rapid coming of Bahá'u'lláh, after the Dispensation of the Báb[1].

Again, with the *sixth* plague we read, "Behold, I come as a thief" (Rev. 16:15). This also has been interpreted as referring to a rapid advent.

In the study of Chapter 11, we found a great earthquake, that which occurred in S̲h̲íráz, native city of the Báb in Irán, after His martyrdom. Upon opening the sixth seal (Rev. 6:12) another mention is found of this earthquake, and we read, "the sun became black as sackcloth of hair". While we have said that the references to celestial bodies are symbols of the religion and its leaders, in this case the prophecy was also fulfilled literally. When the Báb was executed in Tabríz, Irán, a great storm such as had never been seen fell upon the city, darkening the sun all afternoon[2].

It is in the sixth stage that we find the only two references to the Euphrates River, in Rev. 9:14 and Rev. 16:12. These call our attention to Mesopotamia, the region where the first light of the Báb's Revelation dawned.

The Six Stage

It was here in the city of Karbila that two Moslem saints, Shaykh Aḥmad and Siyyid Káẓim, raised their voices in the first years of the XIX century to foretell the dawn of a new day. We read that the water of the Euphrates "was dried up" (Rev. 16:12). Water has always been a symbol of divine knowledge that gives spiritual life. In the region of the Euphrates, the cities of Karbila, Kazimayn and Najaf were theological centers of the Shi'ahs where this water was dispersed, although not now in its pure form. To say that the water "was dried up" means that these Shi'ah teachings, already contaminated with human doctrines, lost their power in the face of the new teachings, in the same manner that water in the desert evaporates when the sun rises. In particular, that which we read next is significant, that the purpose of this phenomenon is,

".... that the way of the kings of the east might be prepared."

These Kings are the Báb and Bahá'u'lláh, who came from Irán, to the east of the Euphrates. This prophecy is explicit in fixing the region in which the new Promised Ones must appear[3].

In one of these references to the Euphrates we find a prophecy that indicates the year of the coming of the Báb, the Prophet of the sixth stage. The prophecy reads:

"And the sixth angel sounded, and I heard a voice from the four horns of the golden alter which is before God, saying to the sixth angel which had the trumpet, Loose the four angels which are bound in the great river Euphrates. And the four angels were loosed, which were prepared for an hour, and a DAY, and a MONTH, and a YEAR for to slay the third part of men." (Rev. 9:13-15)

The calculation of the time mentioned here (discounting the hour as insignificant) is the following:

1 day	1 year
1 month = 30 days	30 years
1 year = 360 days	360 years
Total	391 years

Traditionally, this prophecy has been interpreted by Biblical students as reference to the fall of Constantinople to the forces of the Ottoman Turks in 1453[4]. Constantinople was the seat of the Eastern Orthodox Church and its defeat by the Moslems was interpreted as cutting off "the third part" of the Christians. Counting 391 years forward from 1453, we arrive at 1844 (Figure 1), prophetic year mentioned in many Biblical prophecies as the year of the return of Christ[5].

While the calulations of the Biblical students are correct in pointing to the year 1844, their interpretation does not seem completely in accord with the text of Revelation. The text says that the four angels will be let loose at the end of

The Six Stage

391 years to slay a third part of men. However, the fall of Constantinople occurred at the beginning of the 391 years and therefore can not be interpreted as the death of the third part of men. In this case, what other interpretation can we give to this prophecy?

According to the text, the 391 years ended when the sixth angel sounded his trumpet. This marks the beginnings of the sixth stage and is the initiation of the Dispensation of the Báb, which began in 1844. The period in question did in fact begin 391 years earlier in 1453 with the fall of Constantinople. These years represent the period of the Ottoman Caliphate, from the establishment of the Turkish reign in Constantinople in 1453, until the year 1844 when the Báb appeared and the spiritual forces were liberated that led to the fall of the Caliphate.

We remember that the Ottoman Caliphate was the recognized leadership of the Sunni Moslems and the successor of those who opposed the Imáms (legitimate successors of Muḥammad). In the history of the Sunni sect the Caliphate enjoyed a double sovereignty, one temporal as a civil government and the other spiritual as the leadership of the Sunni Moslems. This double sovereignty declined sharply during the XIX century and finally ended in 1924 when the Caliph Muḥammad VI was ousted by the Young Turk Revolution, thus leaving the Moslems without a spiritual leader.

Revelation 9:14 says that the spiritual forces (represented by four angels) were bound in the

Euphrates River. The valley of the Euphrates was the scene of the greatest tragedies in the history of the Shi'ahs Imáms. The first Imám, Alí, died there in the city of Kufah, and the third Imám, Husayn, whose martyrdom we have described, was assassinated on the plain of Karbila. The Báb himself, in reference to this event said:

> "Erelong We will, in very truth, torment such as waged war against Husayn (Imám Husayn), in the Land of the Euphrates, with the afflictive torment, and the direst and most exemplary punishment"[6]

Identifying the divine punishment promised by the Báb with the fall of the Caliphate, Shoghi Effendi says:

> "The disappearance of the Caliph, the spiritual head of above two hundred million Muhammadans, brought in its wake, in the land that had dealt Islám such a heavy blow, the annulment of the canonical Law, the disendowment of Sunni institutions, the promulgation of a civil Code, the suppression of religious orders, the abrogation of ceremonials and traditions inculcated by the religion of Muhammad"[7]

This is the punishment promised in Revelation 9:16, when the four angels were let loose to kill the third part of men.

We see that the Sunni sect counted at that time with some two hundred million adherents, a

number which corresponds to the size of the army named in Revelation 9:16:
> "And the number of the army of horsemen were two hundred thousand thousand: and I heard the number of them."

However, later we read that it was not by the four angels that the men died, but by the fire, smoke, and brimstone that this army produced. This appears to be a small internal contradiction in Revelation. How can this be explained?

The four angels represent the new Revelation initiated by the Báb and the "fire, smoke, and brimstone" represent the opposition of the Sunni sect and in particular the Caliphate, to the new Revelation. The death to which Revelation refers, in addition to the punishments which we have mentioned, is the spiritual death which mankind brings upon itself by opposing the Promised One of God. This death, which is nothing more nor less than spiritual ignorance, is the punishment which humanity chooses for itself and marks the beginning of unnumbered afflictions.

The third part of men which is mentioned in Revelation possibly refers to the Turkish nation, which was the third nation in the forefront of Islamic history, after the Arabs and Persians. Alternatively, it can refer to the Ottoman Caliphs, who were the third Sunni dynasty that dominated the Middle East, after the Ummayad and the Abbasid.

As to the four angels which brought this punishment, there are at least two possible explanations:

1. When the twelfth and last Imám disappeared in 260 A.H. four men arose successively, saying that the Imám was in hiding and that they would serve as spokesmen between the Hidden Imám and the Shi'ah community. When the fourth of these died, the door of divine guidance remained closed until the Báb appeared in 1844, opening anew the channels of divine guidance. In this sense the four spokesmen were "loosed" with the coming of the Báb.

2. The other explanation is related to the names of the Imáms. Of the twelve Imáms, there are six which are buried in the valley of the Euphrates. They are Alí I, in Najaf; Ḥusayn and Ḥasan II in Karbila; Musa and Muḥammad II in Kazimayn; Alí II in Samarra. In this case, the four angels refer specifically to the Imáms Alí I, Ḥusayn, Muḥammad II, and Alí II. These were "loosed" when the Báb and Bahá'u'lláh appeared, whose names were Alí Muḥammad and Ḥusayn Alí, respectively. That is to say, the four Imáms found new life in the names of the Báb and Bahá'u'lláh as also in their Causes.

For which ever of these explanations that one is inclined, one comes to the same conclusion,

The Six Stage

that the sixth stage is that in which the Cause of the Imáms is vindicated with the coming of the Báb and that the opposers of the Imáms are to suffer a divine punishment. We will find more references to this theme in future chapters. We also learn that the sixth stage is a period of preparation for Armageddon. The nations are gathered for the "battle of that great day of God Almighty" (Revelation 16:14). It is the end of an epoch when the heaven disappears "as a scroll when it is rolled together" (Rev. 6:14).

It is the time of the announcement that "...the great day of his wrath is come" (Rev. 6:17) and of the promise of the "New Jerusalem" and the "new name" (Rev. 3:12). All these represent processes that have their beginning in the sixth stage in the Revelation of the Báb and come to their consummation in the seventh stage, that of Bahá'u'lláh.

REFERENCES

1. 'Abdu'l-Bahá, *Some Answered Questions* p. 56.
2. Shoghi Effendi, *God Passes By* p. 53.
3. See also William Sears, *Thief in the Night* and Appendix 1 of this book.
4. W. Harbert, in *The Coming Battle*, (quoted in William Sears, op. cit., p. 55).
5. William Sears, op. cit. and Appendix 1 of this book.
6. Shoghi Effendi, *The Promised Day is Come,* p. 97.
7. Ibid.

CHAPTER 9

The Seventh Stage

In the letter to the seventh Church we read, "Behold, I stand at the door, and knock" (Rev. 3:20). While in the *sixth* letter the door was promised, in this letter there is *another* who knocks at the door and enters by the door. The Báb was the door and it was Bahá'u'lláh who entered by the door.

There are rather few details to be found in the accounts of the seventh stage. Instead, its prophecies and themes are broad and sweeping. However, summarizing its events, we can say the following. It is a time of climactic resolution, when "there should be time no more" and "the mystery of God should be finished, as he hath declared to his servants the prophets" (Rev. 10:6-7).

It is a time of anger and punishment, of recompense and peace, when "thy wrath is come, and the time of the dead, that they should be judged, and that thou shouldst give reward unto thy servants the prophets, and the saints, and them that fear thy name" (Rev. 11:18), when "the Babylon came in remembrance before God, to give unto her the cup of the wine of the fierceness of his wrath" (Rev. 16:19).

The Seventh Stage

It is the age of final victory, when it is announced that "The kingdoms of this world are become the kingdoms of our Lord and his Christ; and he shall reign for ever and ever... because thou has taken to thee thy great power and has reigned." (Rev. 11:15-17) It is also the time when "the ark of his testament" (Rev. 11:19) appears followed by "lightnings, and voices and thunderings, and an earthquake...." (Rev. 11:19, 8:5 and 16:18). This testament is a reference to the Testament of Bahá'u'lláh[1], which is a unique document in the history of the religions of the world. In His Testament, Bahá'u'lláh clearly designated His eldest Son, 'Abdu'l-Bahá, as His successor and the sole Interpreter of His teachings. By this is meant that the authority within the Bahá'í Faith after Bahá'u'lláh was clearly established.

However, the existence of the Testament of Bahá'u'lláh in the form of a written document was not a guarantee that men would not try to subvert the intentions of Bahá'u'lláh. Just as Jesus had His Judas Iscariote, so did some followers of Bahá'u'lláh betray and rebel against 'Abdu'l-Bahá. The lightnings, voices, thunderings and earth-quakes mentioned in Revelation refer to this rebellion[2]. However, the Testament of Bahá'u'lláh was so clear and explicit that every effort to oppose the legitimate authority of 'Abdu'l-Bahá ended in failure.

It is interesting to consider the significance of the seventh day of creation (Gen. 2:2) in light of the interpretation we have suggested. Supposedly the story of Genesis in the Bible was written by Moses, and Moses also established the seventh day of the week as the Sabbath, to commemorate the seventh day of creation mentioned in Genesis.

According to our study, the days of creation are symbolic of the stages of the spiritual progress of humanity and the seventh day is the climax, the day of peace and rest. From this point of view, we can speculate that the purpose of Moses in establishing the Sabbath (in addition to that of establishing a day of worship), was to commemorate this day (age of peace) which is equivalent to the seventh stage of Revelation, the stage of Bahá'u'lláh.

The Sabbath also is known as the day of the Lord, an apellation which is associated in Biblical prophecies with the time of the end, the final victory of God and the day of universal peace.

Then it is Bahá'u'lláh who has come as the seventh angel to bring the age of peace and universal unity. Many will ask why we have not seen the universal peace if Bahá'u'lláh came more than a century ago? The answer to this question is in the history of the religions of the past. We see that some prophecies are not fulfilled during the lifetime of the Prophet, but later in His Dispensation. For example, in the case of Jesus, the Old Testament says that He who would be born in Bethlehem would be "great unto the ends of the earth" (Micah 5:4). Jesus was born in Bethlehem but during His life

He was not made "great unto the ends of the earth". Rather the prophecy spoke of the entire cycle of the Dispensation of Jesus, during which Jesus became great and renowned throughout the world.

So it is with the prophecies of universal peace, brotherhood and unity. Bahá'u'lláh came as Messenger of God for the present age (the seventh epoch) and within this epoch the promises of peace and unity will be fulfilled. In reality the Writings of Bahá'u'lláh contain the formula for the consummation of these promises and in themselves fulfill the prophecies. This topic deserves much more attention than we will dedicate to it at this moment, but we will return to it in Chapter 14 when we study other prophecies of Revelation related to the reign of peace.

The seven stages which we have studied and the principal signs related with each one are found summarized in Figure 2. These signs will help us to understand the following chapters which make reference to some of the most crucial themes of Revelation: the Millennium, Armageddon, and the New Jerusalem, among others.

Figure 2
The Seven Stages of
Revelation and Their Signs

1. ADAM
   - Promise of the tree of life
   - A fall

2. NOAH
   - Reference to the sea
   - Death and tribulation
3. MOSES
   - The rivers become blood
   - The water is separated from dry land
   - A balance represents the law
4. JESUS
   - Faith, hope and service
   - Power over a fourth of the world
   - Signs in the sun, moon, and stars
5. MUḤAMMAD
   - A beast comes out of the abyss
   - A Dispensation of 1,260 days (1,260 years)
   - Wars and martyrs
6. THE BÁB
   - A great earthquake
   - Spiritual forces from Euphrates river
   - Preparation for Armageddon
7. BAHÁ'U'LLÁH
   - Babylon is overcome
   - Punishment and final victory
   - The Kingdom of Christ established

REFERENCES

1. Shoghi Effendi, *God Passes By* p. 225.
2. Ibid., p. 235.

CHAPTER 10

The Two Prophets of the Modern Epoch

It is a mystery of God that two Divine Messengers have come in this modern age and within a short period of time, and it is impossible to understand all of its implications. We need only contemplate the effects of the coming of Moses and Jesus in Their respective ages, to imagine the spiritual forces unleashed by these two Prophets in rapid succession.

Although contemporaries, the Báb and Bahá'u'lláh never met each other in this world. Their relationship was maintained through correspondence and (we can imagine) through the invisible ties of the spiritual world. However, it should be understood that Their stories are intimately related and that Their Missions are inseparable. The spiritual forces initiated through the Revelation of the Báb found full expression and realization in the successive Revelation of Bahá'u'lláh. For example, the emancipation of women had its first impulse when Ṭáhirih, a woman and a disciple of the Báb, publicly removed her veil from her face, a scandalous act in Islamic society. Later, Bahá'u'lláh ensured the emancipation of women when He proclaimed the equality of men and women. In this and other aspects the Messages and Missions of Bahá'u'lláh and the Báb were complementary.

We will see throughout the remainder of the chapters of Revelation that the Báb and Bahá'u'lláh are represented in a close relationship, reflecting the relationship between their Dispensations.

Throughout the Book of Revelation there are two central figures that dominate the visions. They are the Lamb, and One who is seated on the throne. To discover who these two personages are, we will follow the path of study that we already have used: we will look for relationships between these Two and the seven stages which we have identified. We will see that these two central figures pertain to the sixth and seventh stages.

First, when the sixth seal was opened, the great ones of the earth hide themselves for fear, because the time has come to face the Lamb and He who is seated on the throne. The powerful and mighty...

"... said to the mountains and rocks, Fall on us, and hide us from the face of him that sitteth on the throne, and from the wrath of the Lamb" (Rev. 6:16-17).

And again in the sixth stage we read:

"After this I beheld, and, lo, a great multitude, which no man could number, of all nations, and kindreds, and peoples, and tongues, stood before the throne and before the Lamb clothed with white robes and palms in their hands. And cried with a loud voice, saying, Salvation to our God which sitteth upon the throne and unto the Lamb. (Rev. 7:9-10)

"These are they which came out of great tribulation, and have washed their robes, and made them white in the blood of the Lamb. Therefore are they before the throne of God and serve him day and night in his temple" ... (Rev. 7:14-15)

In the seventh stage we especially find reference to Him who is seated on the throne and to twenty four elders seated around Him.

"And the seventh angel sounded the trumpet... and the four and twenty elders, which sat before God on their seats, fell upon their faces, and worshipped God" (Rev. 11:15-16).

These are the twenty four elders mentioned previously in Chapter 4 that are seated around the throne:

"... behold, a throne was set in heaven, and One sat on the throne..... And round about the throne were four and twenty seats and I saw four and twenty elders sitting...." (Rev. 4:2-4)

We find another reference to the throne in the letter to the seventh Church, Laodicea:

"To him that overcometh will I grant to sit with me in my throne..." (Rev. 3:21)

And with the seventh plague we read:

"And the seventh angel poured out his

vial into the air; and there came a great voice out of the temple of heaven, from the throne, saying, It is done." (Rev. 16:17)

To confirm that it is He on the throne who pronounced these words in the seventh stage, further on we find the same words again:

"And he that sat upon the throne said .... It is done." (Rev. 21:5-6)

These references in the sixth and seventh stages establish a relationship between these stages and the Lamb and the One on the throne. We have already seen that these stages pertain to the Báb and Bahá'u'lláh respectively. Can we conclude that the Lamb and the One on the throne are the Báb and Bahá'u'lláh?

It is obvious that the Lamb has traditionally been thought to refer not to the Báb but to Jesus Christ, and it is clear that the New Testament identifies Jesus as the Lamb of God. If this is true, then why would the author of Revelation have chosen to identify the Báb as the Lamb also? William Sears, Bahá'í writer and author of several books on Bible subjects, has compiled an impressive list of parallels between the lives of Jesus and the Báb[1]. This list is found in the book "Thief in the Night", which is an extensive study of the Biblical prophecies fulfilled by the Báb and Bahá'u'lláh.

Mr. Sears notes the following in regards to Jesus and the Báb:

1. They were both youthful.
2. They were both known for their meekness and loving kindness.

The Two Prophets of The Modern Epoch

3. They both performed healing miracles.
4. The period of their ministry was very brief in each case, and moved with dramatic swiftness to its climax.
5. Both of them boldly challenged time-honored conventions, laws, and rites of the religions into which they had been born.
6. They courageously condemned the unbridled graft and corruption which they saw on every side, both religious and secular.
7. The purity of their own lives shamed the people among whom they taught.
8. Their chief enemies were among the religious leaders of the land. These officials were the instigators of the outrages they were made to suffer.
9. They both had indignities heaped upon them.
10. They were both forcibly brought before the government authorities and were subjected to public interrogation.
11. Both were scourged following this interrogation.
12. They both went, first in triumph then in suffering, through the streets of the city where they were to be slain.
13. They were both paraded publicly, and heaped with humiliation, on the way to their martyrdom.
14. They both spoke words of hope and promise to one who was to die with them; in fact, almost the exact same

words: "Thou shalt be with me in paradise".
15. They were both martyred publicly before the hostile gaze of the onlookers who crowded the scene.
16. A darkness covered the land following their slaying, in each case beginning at noon.
17. Their bodies were both lacerated by soldiers at the time of their slaying.
18. They both remained in ignominious suspension before the eyes of an unfriendly multitude.
19. Their bodies came finally into the hands of their loving followers.
20. When their bodies, in each case, had vanished from the spot where they had been placed, the religious leaders explained away the fact.
21. Only a handful of their followers were with them at the times of their deaths.
22. In each case, one of their chief disciples denied knowing them. This same disciple, in each case, later became a hero.
23. Each of them had an outstanding woman follower who played a dramatic part in making the disciples turn their faces from the past, and look toward the future.
24. Confusion, bewilderment and despair seized their followers, in each case, following their martyrdom.
25. Through their disciples (the Peters and Pauls of each age) their Faiths were carried to all parts of the world.

26. They both replied with the same exact words to the question: Are you the Promised One?
27. Each of them addressed their disciples, charging them to carry their messages to the ends of the earth.

Truly, the parallels between the lives of these two Prophets are impressive, especially those that refer to the details of their martyrdoms. We can suggest that due to the similarities of Their lives and especially because the Báb, as Jesus, shed His blood in the path of God, the Báb also was given the title of "the Lamb".

By a process of elimination, then, we must conclude that Bahá'u'lláh is He who is seated on the throne. We find evidence of this in the book of Ezekiel (1:28), where in a vision the Prophet sees a throne surrounded by four beasts, evidently the same throne as in the vision of John. Ezekiel says that the One on the throne was of the "likeness of the glory of the Lord", that is, the Glory of God, which is the very name of Bahá'u'lláh[2].

An overview of Revelation shows us that He who is seated on the throne is identified with God (Rev. 7:10). Does this mean that the Bahá'ís consider that Bahá'u'lláh is God? No. Bahá'u'lláh Himself explains:

"To every discerning and illumined heart it is evident that God, the unknowable Essence, the divine Being, is immensely exalted beyond every human attribute, such as corporeal existence, ascent and descent, egress and regress. Far be it from His glory that human tongue should adequately recount His praise, or that human heart comprehend His fathomless mystery. He is and hath ever been veiled in the ancient eternity of His Essence, and will remain in His Reality everlastingly hidden from the sight of men. 'No vision taketh in Him, but He taketh in all vision; He is the Subtile, the All-Perceiving.' No tie of direct intercourse can possibly bind Him to His creatures. He standeth exalted beyond and above all separation and union, all proximity and remoteness. No sign can indicate His presence or His absence; inasmuch as by a word of His command all that are in heaven and on earth have come to exist, and by His wish, which is the Primal Will itself, all have stepped out of utter nothingness into the realm of being, the world of the visible"[3].

"The door of the knowledge of the Ancient of Days being thus closed in the face of all beings, the Source of infinite grace, according to His saying: 'His grace hath transcended all things; My grace hath encompassed them all' hath caused those luminous Gems of Holiness to appear out of the realm of the spirit, in the noble form of the human temple, and be made manifest unto all men, that they may impart unto the world the mysteries of the unchangeable Being, and tell of the subtleties of His imperishable Essence. These sanctified Mirrors, these Daysprings of ancient glory are one and all the Exponents on earth of Him Who is the central Orb of the universe, its Essence and ultimate Purpose. From Him proceed their knowledge and power; from Him is derived their sovereignty. The beauty of their countenance is but a reflection of His image, and their revelation a sign of His deathless glory. They are the Treasuries of divine knowledge, and the Repositories of celestial wisdom. Through them is transmitted a grace that is infinite, and by thems revealed the light that can never fade"[4].

That is to say, neither Bahá'u'lláh, nor Jesus, nor any other Prophet is God, but each one has been the sole representative of God on earth in His own Age. Each one has spoken with the voice of God, each one has revealed the Will of God. Each one has been a channel for the Holy Spirit, which is the only tie that unites God with man. In this sense, Bahá'u'lláh says:

"Were any of the all-embracing Manifestations of God to declare: 'I am God!' He verily speaketh the truth, and no doubt attacheth there to."[5]

That is to say, each Prophet is God in that God reveals Himself to man in the being of the Prophet. Do we find any Biblical basis for this interpretation? Yes!

To Moses God said: "... thou shalt be to him (Aaron) instead of God." (Exo. 4:16)

Jesus also identified the "gods" as the Revealers of the Word of God. Jesus said:

> "Is it not written in your law, I said, Ye are gods? If he called them GODS, unto WHOM THE WORD OF GOD CAME..." (John 10:34-35)

Jesus refers to a passage of Psalms:

> "I have said, Ye are gods; and all of you are children of the most High. But ye shall die like men and fall like one of the princes" (Psalms 82: 6-7).

That is, the "gods" that "die like men" are those "unto whom the Word of God came". They are the Revealers of the Word of God, the Prophets. In reality, God has come to the world in the Revelation of each Prophet (see Gen. 50:24 and Exo. 4:31 in reference to Moses, and Báb. 3:3 in reference to Muḥammad). However, the Bible promises that "God Himself will come" (Is. 35:4) and Jesus prophesies the coming of the Father in His parable of the vineyard (Mark 12). What can we conclude them? Has Bahá'u'lláh fulfilled these promises of the coming of God Himself, or not?

Certainly Bahá'u'lláh has fulfilled these prophecies. In the Biblical prophecies, the Revelation of Bahá'u'lláh has been distinguished as the coming of God Himself, because His Revelation represents the most complete Revelation of God that the world has ever known. This is the Revelation to which Jesus referred when He said:

"I have yet many things to say unto you, but ye cannot bear them now. Howbeit when he, the SPIRIT OF TRUTH, is come, he will guide you into ALL TRUTH: for he shall not speak of himself; but whatsoever he shall hear, that shall he speak..." (John 16:12-13)

Many interpret the Spirit of Truth to be the Holy Spirit speaking through the Apostles. However, none of the Apostles gave this interpretation, neither did they say that they had finished revealing "All Truth". On the contrary, the Apostles themselves foretold a great Revelation of the divine truth in the future and an event of such weight as the revelation of "All Truth" seems to be reserved for the last days (Rev. 5:1-9; Rev. 20:12; Dan. 12:9).

Further, insomuch as Jesus said that this Spirit "shall not speak of himself; but whatsoever he shall hear, that shall he speak," this shows that the Spirit of Truth is a man, who will speak that with which God inspires him. The Bahá'ís believe that Bahá'u'lláh is the Spirit of Truth and His Revelation, according to the testimony of Jesus, is the most complete which God has given the world. It is for this reason that the Bible makes reference to the coming of Bahá'u'lláh as the coming of God Himself and in Revelation, Bahá'u'lláh is represented as God seated on His throne.

At this point, the Christian reader might well have an important question: What relationship do the Báb and Bahá'u'lláh have with the return of

Christ? It is appropriate to answer this question now.

In the *Book of Certitude* Bahá'u'lláh speaks extensively about the mystery of the return, and the Bible student will want to refer to these passages. For our purposes we will refer to an example from the pages of the Gospel, and it is this.

Jesus was born in a time of vivid Messianic expectations and those versed in the Mosaic Law recited daily the signs of the coming Messiah. Among these were clear promises of the return of the Prophet Elias to announce the coming of the Promised One. The Prophet Elias shares with Jesus the distinction of having ascended to heaven, thus escaping death. Therefore, the Jews surely expected with confidence that Elias would return in his corporal form, just as the Christians today await the return of Jesus in the same flesh which disappeared from the view of the Apostles 2,000 years ago.

Apparently the Scribes quoted this requirement to the disciples, since they came before Jesus to ask Him to explain the apparent nonfulfillment of the prophecy. Jesus answered them:

> "Elias truly shall first come, and restore all things. But I say unto you that Elias is come already and they knew him not, but have done unto him whatsoever they listed..... then the disciples understood that he spoke unto them of John the Baptist." (Mat. 17:11-13)

It is obvious in this Biblical text that John the Baptist fulfilled that for which the Jews were waiting.

However, the interpretation of Jesus is in contrast with that which John himself said, when the priests asked him, "Art thou Elias?" John answered: "I am not" (John 1:21).

This seems to be a contradiction between the words of Jesus and those of John. How can we resolve the contradiction? And in what sense was John the return of Elias?

It is clear that John was not Elias in flesh such as the Jews expected (therefore John told the priests, "I am not"). Elias did not return materially nor with the same name. The return of Elias in John was rather in a *spiritual* sense!

Just as Elias came in a time in which the Mosaic Law had been corrupted and the Israelites had forgotten Jehovah, so did John. Elias reproached the Israelites fervently for their negligence before God, bringing upon themselves afflictions and suffering; John did the same. Elias lived a life in the desert, solitary and comfortless; John also. As John came with the same mission as Elias and manifested the same qualities of spiritual purity and religious fervor, it is said that John came in the spirit of Elias.

The corollary of the argument that the return of Elias was symbolic and spiritual, is that his ascension to heaven was also symbolic of an ascension to spiritual worlds superior to this material kingdom.

Returning to the theme of the return of Christ we can extrapolate the case of Elias and

John to the relationship between Jesus and the Báb and Bahá'u'lláh.

In Chapter 3 we said that all the major Prophets, such as Noah, Moses, and Jesus, have held a station far above the rest of humanity, the station which we know as the Holy Spirit. In so much as the Holy Spirit (or Christ Spirit) has returned to shine in this world in the persons of the Báb and Bahá'u'lláh, it is said that They fulfill the prophecies for the return of Christ. However, for we puny human beings, the Holy Spirit is rather a title for a Universal Reality, an Infinite Essence that is far above our comprehension and capacity. We know the Holy Spirit for its effects and qualities which appear in those Holy Beings which are the source of life for the world. The perfections of Christ, His wisdom, His patience, His love which forgave all and transcends this poor world of ours, these are some of the evidences of the Holy Spirit.

While it is correct to say that the Holy Spirit has returned in the Báb and Bahá'u'lláh, what this means to us, within the reaches of our poor comprehension, is that the same spiritual evidences that were manifested in Jesus Christ, have again manifested themselves in these two Prophets of modern time. In this sense, the Báb and Bahá'u'lláh are the return of Christ, the same as John the Baptist was the return of Elias.

Precisely, Bahá'u'lláh is the return of Christ in the Glory of the Father.

In this sense, Revelation 3:12, where we find words referring to the return of Christ, is very significant:

"Him that overcometh .... I will write upon him my new name."

Here the promise of a new name is explicit; just as Elias returned with a new name, Christ did also.

REFERENCES

1. Shoghi Effendi has commented on the parallels between the lives of Jesus Christ and the Báb, *God Passes By* p. 56-57.
2. The author is grateful to Mr. Phillip Turner for this observation.
3. Bahá'u'lláh, *Book of Certitude* p. 98.
4. Ibid, pp. 99-100.
5. Ibid, p. 178.

CHAPTER 11

The Remaining Chapters of Revelation: Analysis

We know now that the seven stages of Revelation are described in a cyclic form and therefore the events of Revelation are not strictly chronological. Each series of seven events represents the same seven spiritual epochs which are repeated with different accounts and details, but with enough in common to recognize a pattern.

When we begin to study the visions of the remaining chapters of Revelation, we will see that these also are repetitive. They are not in chronological order either, rather they also repeat the same events several times, with different symbols and details. What is more, we will see that they are related to the seven stages with which we are already familiar.

How can we analyze these visions, apparently not in any special order, to be able to understand them? We already have the tools to do so:

    1. We have a "Master Plan", which is the scheme of the seven stages.

The Remaining Chapters of Revelation: Analysis

2. We have certain keys or symbols which pertain to one or another of the seven stages.
3. We have a methodology: we will compare the remaining visions with the seven stages and establish relationships with them, by means of the keys and symbols.

When we studied the seven stages, we noted that, at the time when Revelation was revealed, the first four stages had already come to pass and only the visions of the last three stages were truly prophetic. For this reason the events pertaining to the fifth, sixth and seventh stages are described in more detail. We will soon see that the rest of the visions which we are going to study pertain to the last three stages.

First, we will review Chapter 11 briefly, to remind ourselves of the keys and symbols which will help us in the following analysis, and the sequence in which they occur. In Chapter 11, we read:

1. a) The Holy City was given over to the gentiles for 42 months (1,260 dias = 1,260 years)
   b) There are two Witnesses (Prophets) who offer their testimony for 1,260 days (years). These are Muḥammad and his successor, 'Ali.'
   c) The beast comes out of the abyss to make war on the two Witnesses. This is the opposition of the Umayyad.
   d) Their bodies lie in the street for 3½ days (1.260 years). This means that the

religion of Muḥammad would be as a corpse, due to the opposition of the beast.

Up to verse 10, Chapter 11 speaks of the Dispensation of Muḥammad. With verse 11 we begin to find references to the Báb.

2. a) After 3½ days the bodies stand up on their feet. These represent the Báb and His foremost disciple, Quddús.
   b) The two ascend to heaven in view of their enemies, that is, the two were martyred.
   c) The second "woe" has passed and the third comes quickly.

This last verse signals the end of the Dispensation of the Báb and the beginning of that of Bahá'u'lláh.

3. a) The seventh trumpet sounds.
   b) Twenty four elders bow in adoration before the One on the throne. We have already seen that He on the throne is Bahá'u'lláh.
   c) God takes the power to reign.
   d) It is time of the judgement of the dead and the destruction of evil.
   e) The Testament is revealed and there are lightnings, thunders, voices, and earthquakes. These represent the opposition to 'Abdu'l-Bahá, the Successor of Bahá'u'lláh named in the Testament.

This sequence of events which is related to the Dispensations of Muḥammad, the Báb and

Bahá'u'lláh, is basically the same sequence that is repeated in Chapter 12, where we find the following:

1. A woman appears clothed with the sun, with the moon under her feet and upon her head a crown of twelve stars. She is with child and threatened by a *dragon* that has seven heads and ten horns. The woman takes refuge in the desert for 1.260 days.

In so much as the text speaks of a dragon (a beast) and of a period of 1,260 days (1,260 years), it is clear that these verses refer to the Dispensation of Muḥammad.

2. A child is born and ascends to heaven.

This corresponds to that which we read of the Báb in Chapter 11 and refers to His martyrdom.

3. Michael comes to war against the dragon and overcomes him. The Kingdom of God is proclaimed.

The victory and the Kingdom of God pertain to the stage of Bahá'u'lláh.

When we read Chapters 17 to 19, we find the sequence is repeated again:

1. A harlot is seen seated upon a beast in the desert. Again the beast has seven heads and ten horns. The harlot is drunk with blood of the martyrs.

The mention of the beast with seven heads and ten horns again establishes a relationship with the opposition to Muḥammad. Also, we see mention of the martyrs, which we have suggested are related to Islám.

2. The beast makes war against the Lamb.

We have already seen that the Lamb in Revelation is the Báb.

3. An angel with great glory comes, who judges the harlot and the beast. The wedding feast of the Lamb is prepared.

The epoch of judgement is the epoch of Bahá'u'lláh.

The sequence is repeated one last time in Chapters 20 to 22:

1. Again there is mentioned the dragon, the abyss and the martyrs.

These references pertain to the Dispensation of Muḥammad.

2. Satan is let loose after a thousand years to call the peoples to the great battle (Armageddon).

We saw in Chapter 16 of Revelation that the call to Armageddon pertains to the sixth stage, that of the Báb.

3. One appears seated on a throne, who comes to judge the dead. Death and hell are overcome. There comes a new heaven, a new earth and the New Jerusalem. The betrothed of the Lamb is prepared as a bride.

We already know that Bahá'u'lláh is He who is seated on the throne and whose epoch is that of judgement and the final victory.

The Remaining Chapters of Revelation: Analysis

These sequences are summarized in Table 2, which will serve the reader to orient himself in the detailed study of the chapters which follow.

TABLE 2
A Summary of Some Events of Revelation that are Related with Muḥammad, the Báb, and Bahá'u'lláh

Chapters	Chapter 11	Chapter 12	Chapters 17-19	20-22
MUḤAM-MAD	11:1-10 Holy City trodden on 42 months	12:1-4 A woman clothed with the sun and the moon and 12 stars; she is pregnant.	17:1-3 In the desert there is a harlot called Babylon seated upon the beast of 7 heads and 10 horns. The harlot is drunk with blood of martyrs.	20:1-6 The serpent (satan) is bound in the abyss
	Two witnesses testify 1,260 days (years) The beast from the abyss makes war against them and overcomes them.	She is threatened by a serpent with 7 heads and 10 horns that attacks 1/3 of the stars. She takes refuge in the desert for 1,260 days. The woman is in refuge 3 times.		There are martyrs that They live and reign 1,000 years
	Bodies lie 3 days (1,260 years)			
THE BÁB	11:11-14 After 3 days they raise to their feet and ascend to heaven. There is a great earthquake. 2nd woe is past and 3rd woe comes quickly.	12:5 A child is born and ascends to heaven.	17:14 The harlot and beast make war on the Lamb.	20:7-10 Satan is let loose to summon the nations.

	11:15-19	12:7-13	18:1-19:10	20:11-22,23
	7th trumpet sounds; 24 Elders worship God; He takes the power to reign.	Michael wars against the serpent and overcomes him.	An angel comes in great glory.	There is one seated on a throne; the dead are judged.
BAHÁ' U' LLÁH	It is time of the judgement of the dead and of the destruction of evil. The Testament is revealed. There are lightning, voices, thunder and earthquakes.	The kingdom of God is established.	The harlot of Babylon is judged with the beast. The wedding of the Lamb is prepared.	Death and hell are overcome. New heaven, new earth, New Jerusalem that is the bride of the Lamb.

CHAPTER 12

Chapter 12 of Revelation: The Woman and the Beast

The first thing we observe in Chapter 12 is that it is a cyclic account in itself. A woman is represented who is threatened by a dragon. The woman flees from the dragon and takes refuge in the desert for 1,260 days. We find this scene in verses 1 to 6 and it is repeated later in verse 14, where 1,260 days are represented as "a time, times and a half". That is, "one time" is one year, "times" are two years, and "half" a time is a half of a year. Added together, these give 3½ years or 1,260 days according to Biblical calculations. We have already seen that 1,260 days (1,260 years) denote the duration of the Dispensation of Muḥammad. What, then, does this vision represent?

Rev. 12.1 says that there is "a woman clothed with the sun with the moon under her feet and on her head a crown of twelve stars". The woman, say the Bahá'í Writings, represents the sacred Law of God — in this case the law revealed by Muḥammad[1]. The sun and the moon represent the two great Empires of Persia and

Turkey, whose national symbols are the sun and the moon, respectively. These two Empires were subject to the Law of Islám, the religion of Muḥammad.

Who do the stars represent?

When we studied Chapter 8 of Revelation within the context of the third stage, we associated a star that fell from heaven with a man. These twelve stars are also men, but holy men, the twelve Imáms (successsors of Muḥammad).

It says, "And she being with child cried", that is, the Law of God suffered great problems until the perfect offspring was produced. This son was the Promised One of the Law of Islám, the Báb.

> "And there appeared another wonder in heaven; and behold a great red dragon, having seven heads and ten horns...." (Rev. 12:3).

We have said that the beast represents the dynasties which opposed the legitimate successors to Muḥammad and with respect to this dragon, the Bahá'í Writings give us more details. The ten horns represent the ten names of the leaders of the Umayyad. Some names are repeated in the persons of successive leaders, but the ten names are:

1. Abu-Sufyan
2. Mu'awiyah (I and II)
3. Yazid (I, II and III)
4. Marwan (I and II)
5. 'Abdu'l-Malik
6. Al-Walid (I and II)
7. Sulayman
8. 'Umar
9. Hisham
10. Ibrahim.

Chapter 12 of Revelation

The seven heads represent the seven domains of the Umayyad: Syria, Persia, Arabia, Egypt, North Africa, Spain and Turkey.

This dragon threw down "the third part of the stars" with his tail, (Rev. 12:4). This means that the Umayyad were responsible for the assassination of several of the Imáms (stars) which succeeded Muḥammad.

Later we see that the dragon threatened the man child as soon as it was born. We have said that the man child is the Báb and we find here that He was taken up to heaven, just as the Báb was in Rev. 11:12, where it says He ascended "up to heaven in a cloud".

In verse 6 we read that the woman took refuge in the desert for 1,260 days. This refers to the desert of Hijaz in the Western Arabia, the native land of Muḥammad. That is, for the 1,260 days (years) of the Dispensation of Muḥammad, the desert of Hijaz was the refuge of the Law of God.

Verses 7 to 13 tell the story of the final victory over the dragon. We know that He who comes after the Báb (the man child of verse 5) to win the final victory is Bahá'u'lláh. There are few details about this victory in chapter 12, but what is interesting is that the *name* given to Him who defeats the dragon: His name is *Michael*. This is the only reference to Michael in Revelation, but there are other prophecies about Him in the book of Daniel:

"And at that time shall Michael stand up, the great prince..." (Dan. 12:1)

"But the prince of the kingdom of Persia withstood me one and twenty days: but, lo, Michael, one of the chief princes, came to help me" (Dan. 10:13).

Here we see that Michael is "one of the chief princes" of Persia. We know that Bahá'u'lláh was born in Persia. He was of a family of the nobility of Persia and a descendant of kings, one of the "chief princes". Furthermore, those who opposed Bahá'u'lláh most fervently were the Moslem clergy and the king (prince) of the Persian kingdom.

These prophecies of Daniel confirm that Michael in Revelation is Bahá'u'lláh.

REFERENCES

1. 'Abdu'l-Bahá, *Some Answered Questions*, pp. 67-72.

CHAPTER 13

Chapters 17 to 19: The Harlot and Her Judgement

These chapters are very similar to Chapter 12, and the symbols that we studied in that chapter will serve us to understand the symbols that we find here. First, the vision begins in the wilderness:
"So he carried me away in the spirit into the wilderness" (Rev. 17:3).

In 12 : 6 we identified this wilderness (or desert) as Hijíz in Arabia, where the drama of Muḥammad took place.

There in the wilderness John saw a harlot seated on a beast of seven heads and ten horns. In Chapter 12 we learned that these are the seven domains and ten names of the Umayyad, the opponents of Muḥammad. The text of Chapter 17 confirms this interpretation because it says that the seven heads are seven mountains (geographical regions) (Rev. 17:9) and the ten horns are ten kings (that is, their names) (Rev. 17:12).

The harlot is "drunken with the blood of the saints" (Rev. 17:6). We have seen how the enemies of Muḥammad slew Ḥusayn, His grandson, and celebrated his martyrdom savagely.

We read of the beast that:

"The beast that thou sawest was, and is not; and shall ascend out of the bottomless pit, and go into perdition" (Ref. 17:8).

This verse refers to the forces of opposition which existed in the time of Muḥammad, which subsided for a while, and which rose up again in the time of the Báb. We read that they will:

"make war with the Lamb, and the Lamb shall overcome them" (Rev. 17:14).

As we know, this Lamb is the Báb. In Chapter 12 also we say that the ancient forces of opposition (the beast) threatened the Báb and we will find the same when we study Chapter 20.

We have stated that the horns and heads of the beast represent kings and dominions. What then does the harlot that is associated with the beast represent?[1]

In Chapter 12 we found a holy woman that represented the sacred Law of God. The harlot, on the other hand, is a corrupt woman associated with opposition to Muḥammad and represents corrupt doctrine. The harlot is seated over waters which are "peoples, and multitudes, and nations, and tongues" (Rev. 17:15). The fact that she is seated over these represents a spiritual oppression of the minds and souls of

The Harlot and Her Judgement

men by the corrupt doctrine. "The truth shall make you free" (John 8:32), but the corrupt doctrine submerges men in superstition and darkness.

In Rev. 17:18 it says that the harlot is the "great city, which reigneth over the kings of the earth." We see that frequently in the Bible a woman is compared with a city and vice versa. For example, Rev. 21:2 refers to "the Holy City, New Jerusalem ... prepared as a bride". Later we will discuss this as another symbol of the Law of God. Here in Chapter 17 we find the corrupt doctrine represented as a harlot and also as the "great city" called Babylon.

It is interesting to explore why the harlot is called *BABYLON*. Historically, Babylon was an enemy of Israel and its crime was having destroyed the temple of Solomon and trodden on Jerusalem some centuries before Christ. In Chapter 11 we read of another Holy City that is trodden under foot[2].

"Rise, and measure the temple of God, and the altar, and them that worship therein. But the court which is without the temple leave out, and measure it not; for it is given unto the Gentiles: *and the Holy City shall they tread under foot forty and two months*" (Rev. 11:1-2).

We said before that the period of forty-two months mentioned in the verse above refers to the 1,260 lunar years of the Dispensation of Muḥammad, and from this we deduce that the prophecy refers to the history of Islám. What does Babylon have to do with the Holy City mentioned here? Just as ancient Babylon destroyed and trampled on ancient Jerusalem, so did symbolic Babylon destroy and trample on symbolic Jerusalem during the 1,260 years of the Islamic Dispensation, as is described in Rev. 11:2.

Babylon is the corrupt doctrine of those who opposed Muḥammad and the twelve Imáms, the doctrine that destroyed and abused the Holy City (Law of God) of Muḥammad. Today this doctrine lives in the Sunni sect. These relationships are represented in the following Figure[3].

Chapter 18 begins with the descent of an angel from heaven. Insomuch as this angel (Prophet) has "descended from heaven" (Rev. 18:1), it is apparent that it refers to a Prophet of the station of Jesus who also said "I came down from heaven" (John 6:38).

"and the earth was lightened with his GLORY" (Rev. 18:1).

That is, the world was illumined and educated by this Prophet. This is Bahá'u'lláh, the GLORY OF GOD, who comes to judge Babylon, declaring:

"Babylon the great is fallen, is fallen" (Rev. 18:2)

All of Chapter 18 and a part of chapter 19 are dedicated to the judgement of Babylon. In that Babylon represents the Sunni doctrine, its judgement represents the punishment of Sunni Islám, such as was discussed in chapter 8 where we learned of prophecies about the fall of

The Harlot and Her Judgement

the Caliphate. In a broader sense, it appears that Babylon is associated in this modern age with commercialism and materialism which are the spirit of the age in which we live and the new corrupt doctrine. We see that it is the merchants who lament over the fall of Babylon:

FIGURE 3.
Relationship between Various Symbols of Revelation used to Represent the Law of God in the Dispensation of Muḥammad

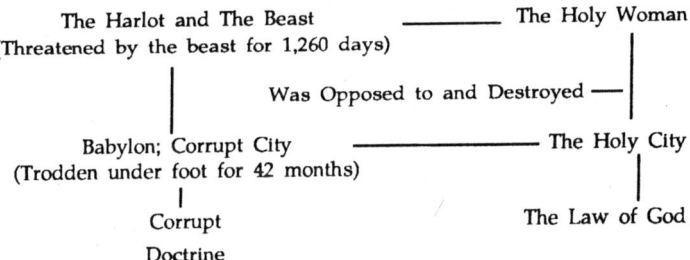

"And the merchants of the earth shall weep and mourn over her; for no man buyeth their merchandise any more" (Rev. 18:11).

That which is repeated many times in Chapter 18 is the rapidness of the fall:

"Therefore shall her plagues come in one day" (Rev. 18:8)

"...for in one hour is thy judgment come." (Rev. 18:10)

"For in one hour so great riches is come to naught." (Rev. 18:17)

"For in one hour is she made desolate."

(Rev. 18:19)

Bahá'u'lláh, warning humanity of an imminent disaster which is to come, has said:

"The world is in travail, and its agitation waxeth day by day. Its face is turned towards waywardness and unbelief. Such shall be its plight, that to disclose it now would not be meet and seemly. Its perversity will long continue. And when the appointed hour is come, there shall suddenly appear that which shall cause the limbs of mankind to quake. Then, and only then, will the Divine Standard be unfurled, and the Nightingale of Paradise warble its melody."[3]

"O ye peoples of the world! Know, verily, that an unforseen calamity is following you, and that grievous retribution awaiteth you. Think not the deeds ye have committed have been blotted from My sight."[4]

"Say: O ye that are bereft of understanding! A severe trial pursueth you, and will suddenly overtake you."[5]

"Soon shall the blasts of His chastisement beat upon you, and the dust of hell enshroud you. Those men who, having amassed the vanities and ornaments of the earth, have turned away disdainfully from God — these have lost both this world and the world to come. Ere long, will God, with the Hand of Power, strip them of their possessions, and divest them

The Harlot and Her Judgement

of the robe of His bounty. To this they themselves shall soon witness. Thou, too, shalt testify.

Say: O people! Let not this life and its deceits deceive you, for the world and all that is therein is held firmly in the grasp of His Will. He bestoweth His favor on whom He willeth, and from whom He willeth He taketh it away. He doth whatsoever He chooseth. Had the world been of any worth in His sight, He surely would never have allowed His enemies to possess it, even to the extent of a grain of mustard seed. He hath, however, caused you to be entangled with its affairs, in return for what your hands have wrought in His Cause. This, indeed, is a chastisement which ye, of your own will, have inflicted upon yourselves, could ye but perceive it. Are ye rejoicing in the things which, according to the estimate of God, are contemptible and worthless, things wherewith He proveth the hearts of the doubtful?"[6]

After the judgement of Babylon, Chapter 19 speaks of the marriage of the Lamb but here we find few details. We will return to this theme when we study chapter 21.

Chapter 19 closes with a vision of two Holy Beings. One is an angel which is standing in the sun (Rev. 19;17). This angel calls everyone to the final judgement of the world and we saw before that this call is related to the Dispensation of the Báb. In Chapter 12 we saw that the sun was a symbol of the Persian Empire. The fact that this angel is standing in the sun refers to the appearance of the Báb in Persia.

The other Holy Being is seated upon a white horse (Rev. 19:11) and comes to judge the "beast and the kings of the earth" with a sword which comes from His mouth (Rev. 19:15), that is to say, with His Word. This Holy Being is Bahá'u'lláh. The judgement of the kings of the earth is too long of a story to treat in detail here. Briefly, Bahá'u'lláh directed letters to the kings of Persia, Turkey, and Europe, reprimanding them for their militaristic policies and commanding them to establish peace. When these rejected and ridiculed the call of Bahá'u'lláh, He foretold the fall of those kings and the horrible wars which destroyed their empires. The reader should study the book *The Promised Day Has Come*, by Shoghi Effendi, for more details.

REFERENCES

1. Many scholars who have interpreted Revelation historically in terms of the immediate situation of the Primitive Church, believe that the harlot represents ancient Rome, because it is described as a great city seated upon seven mountains.
2. 'Abdu'l-Bahá has explained further that the temple and the altar refer to the fundamental and spiritual basis of the Law of God and represent divine qualities such as faith, knowledge, justice, love, peace, and humility. These qualities are the

center of the Law of God and are eternal and common to all religions. The Holy City which is outside represents the exterior forms of the religion, such as rites and ceremonies and social laws. When the inner spirit of the religion has died, only the exterior forms (the courtyard and the city which is outside) remain, and these are held in the hands of the clergy (represented as the gentiles). The same occurred with the Judaic religion in the time of Jesus.
3. Bahá'u'lláh, *Gleanings from the Writings of Bahá'u'lláh*, p. 118.
4. Ibid, p. 209.
5. Ibid, p. 169.
6. Ibid, p. 209.

CHAPTER 14

Chapters 20 to 22: The Millennium; The New Jerusalem

Chapters 20 to 22 repeat in more detail the same sequence of events that we have seen in previous chapters and contain the most dramatic visions of Revelation. In particular, the vision of Chapter 20 is one of the most cited in the Apocalyptic doctrine of the churches because it concerns the millennium when the saints will reign with Christ. It will be a surprise for most Christians to find that this event in which they have centered their hopes for the future, has already passed! We will see, however, that it was fulfilled in the Dispensation of Muḥammad.

First, we see that there is mention of the dragon and this is an indication that the chapter refers to the Dispensation of Muḥammad. Furthermore, we read that:

"... when the thousand years are expired, Satan shall be loosed out of his prison, And shall go out to deceive the nations which are in the four quarters of the earth, Gog and Magog, to gather them together to battle: the number of whom is as the sand of the sea." (Rev. 20:7-8)

The Millennium; The New Jerusalem

The battle mentioned here is Armageddon since in Ezekiel 38 and 39 we learn that Gog is a prince and Magog is a kingdom that would participate in the battle of Armageddon in the time in which the Jews had returned to the Holy Land (the present time).

Today Christians all over the world, observing that the Jews have returned, believe Armageddon is imminent and they are right. But according to Rev. 20:7-8, the battle of Armageddon with Gog and Magog comes AFTER the millennium. If Armageddon is near, this means that the millennium has already passed!

Also, we saw in Rev. 16:16 that the call to the battle of Armageddon is related to the sixth stage, the epoch of the Báb which began in 1844. If the call to Armageddon in 1844 ended the millennium (Rev. 20:7), this places the millennium in the Dispensation of Muḥammad — that which proceeded the Dispensation of the Báb.

What then, is the relationship between Muḥammad and the millennium? We read in Rev. 20:4 that those who reign with Christ during the thousand years are martyrs *"beheaded for the testimony of Jesus"*. When we studied the 5th Stage, we saw that the martyrs mentioned there were martyrs of the Cause of Muḥammad and here in Chapter 20 we find more evidence of the same, due to the form of their death: they are beheaded.

We already know that, in the history of Islám, this was precisely the fate of Ḥusayn, grandson of Muḥammad, and his companions, who were slain on the plain of Karbila. The body of Ḥusayn was mutilated and his head carried as a trophy on the point of a lance by his assassins.

The same chapter says that the martyrs "lived and reigned with Christ a thousand years". The martyrs were Ḥusayn and the other eleven Imáms, the true successors of Muḥammad. To say that they reigned a thousand years means that they shared the spiritual authority with Christ for a thousand years. We remember that the line of succession of the Imáms ended in the year 260 of the Moslem calendar and the Dispensation of Muḥammad lasted until the year 1,260. There were precisely one thousand lunar years from the disappearance of the last Imám till the end of the Muḥammadan epoch and for those thousand years the spiritual authority was shared by the Imáms and "Christ". In this case, "Christ" refers to Muḥammad because each Prophet is the Christ (Messiah) of His age.

Rev. 20:5 says: "This is the first resurrection". The word resurrection does not refer to the revival of corpses, but to the revival of souls, of society, and of religion. It is a spiritual revival and in the *Book of Certitude* Bahá'u'lláh explains that there has been a resurrection in each new Dispensation. To say "this is the first resurrection" means that this is the first new Dispensation after that of Jesus.

The authority of the Imáms as successors of Muḥammad is recognized by the Shi'ah sect of

The Millennium; The New Jerusalem

the Moslems, that which prevailed in Irán (Persia). It was in Persia where the Imáms "reigned" for a thousand years until 1,260 A.H. The establishment of their authority and the overcoming of the forces of opposition, at least in Persia, is represented as the overcoming of Satan for a thousand years (Rev. 20:1-3).

> "And when the thousand years are expired, Satan will be loosed from his prison", (Rev. 20:7).

That is to say, in the year 1,260 A.H. (1844 A.D.) with the appearance of the Báb, the ancient forces of opposition would be awakened again, this time in the land of Persia among the same Shi'ahs who before defended the authority of the Imáms.

> "And (Satan) shall go out to deceive the nations which are in the four corners of the earth, Gog and Magog, to gather them together to battle" (Rev. 20:8).

We have seen that this is the call to the battle of Armageddon, that which is associated with the sixth stage, the stage of the Báb (Rev. 16:16).

> "And they went up on the breadth of the earth, and compassed the camp of the saints" (Rev. 20:9).

The followers of the Báb took refuge in an improvised fort called the Fort of Ṭabarsí, and the army pursued and surrounded them leaving few survivors. Quddus, the foremost disciple of the Báb whose martyrdom was foreseen in Chapter 11 of Revelation, died there. Other Bábis died as heroes in Nayriz; others in Zanjan. Their stories are found in the book *Dawnbreakers*.

Thus we see that the period of one thousand years mentioned in Rev. 20 transpired during the Dispensation of Muḥammad. It is appropriate at this point to make a slight digression from our theme to speak of the millennium. The word "millennium" literally means, "thousand years". However, over the centuries, the "millennium" has taken on a much broader significance than a simple period of time; in Christian theology, the millennium represents the Reign of God on earth, together with all the characteristics normally associated with it: justice, peace, brotherhood, and the victory of good over evil. Many of the prophecies of the Old Testament have been associated with this expected millennium.

Now, in Revelation the "millennium" per se is not mentioned, but rather the reign of Christ that will last a thousand years. In reality, the description of those thousand years is very brief and the events related to this period are the imprisonment of Satan and the resurrection of the saints beheaded for the testimony of Christ. We have now seen that these events were fulfilled within the Dispensation of Muḥammad. The other events frequently associated with the millennium in the doctrine of the church, such as the reign of peace and justice, are not to be found in Revelation 20:1-7. Their relationship with these verses has been an inference of theologians. This promised world of peace and justice is not part of the Dispensation of

The Millennium; The New Jerusalem

Muḥammad, but rather comes *after* the millennium of Revelation 20 in the epoch of Bahá'u'lláh.

Then, should we conclude that the reign of peace is NOT part of the millennium? Not necessarily. The Christian theologian, W.T. Blackstone, comments on the significance of the number "7" in Jewish literature[1]. According to Dr. Blackstone, the Jews considered that history is divided into seven stages (epochs) of one thousand years each. The Jews related the seventh epoch or millennium, with the reign of peace and with the Sabbath, *the day* (or epoch) of rest, just as we have discussed before. This doctrine is very close to the interpretation which we have given to the seven stages of Revelation. Furthermore, according to this point of view, history is a *series* of millenniums. The millennium of Revelation 20 is related to Muḥammad, and the seventh millennium with Bahá'u'lláh and the reign of peace.

In the holy books we find more references to support this interpretation, for example: the Disciple Peter reminds us that "with the Lord, a day is as a thousand years" (2 Peter 3:8).

In the Qurán, Muḥammad also prophesied "a day whose duration will be a thousand years" — a prophecy which reminds us of the millennium of Rev. 20. Shoghi Effendi stated that the end of this day of a thousand years corresponded with the advent of the Báb[2], in the same way as we have interpreted Rev. 20.

Bahá'u'lláh Himself, referring to the renewal of the Word of God through the Divine Prophets says:

> "Once in about a thousand years shall this City (the word of God) be renewed and readorned"[3]

The Dispensations of some Prophets have been more than one thousand years and others less. But, according to Biblical calculation, the period from Adam till the present covers approximately six millenniums. Bahá'u'lláh has brought the seventh millennium, the "Golden Millennium", within which will be established the reign of peace and justice. We will read about this reign in Chapters 21 and 22.

Continuing with the events described in Chapter 20, again there appears One who comes to defeat the forces of evil.

> "And I saw a great white throne, and him that sat on it, from whose face the earth and the heaven fled away" (Rev. 20:11)

We have related him seated on the "white throne" with the seventh stage and with Bahá'u'lláh. Again, we see that this is the epoch to judge the dead.

> "and the dead were judged out of those things which were written in the books" (Rev. 20:12).

In this case the dead are not the corporally dead, but spiritually dead. The dead are those who are unconscious of God, who reject those sent by Him, and who persecute the Saints. As Jesus said: "Let the dead bury the dead."

The Millennium; The New Jerusalem

A very simple statement in Revelation 20:12 is highly significant.

"And the books were opened"

This prophecy, apparently so simple, implies much. In itself it is the fulfillment of a promise made to Daniel many years before:

"And he said, Go thy way, Daniel: for the words are closed up and sealed till the time of the end." (Daniel 12:9)

The act of "opening the books" refers to the opening of their meanings and mysteries, that is, to explain the mysteries of the holy books of the past — the Bible, the Qurán, the Baghavad Gita, and others. If we read these books literally, they seem to be contradictory and impossible to reconcile. But if we understand the spiritual meanings and symbols that are used, we see that all speak of the same message — only with different symbols. The *Book of Certitude*, to which we have referred, is the key for opening the mysteries of the Holy Books. In it Bahá'u'lláh explains the symbolic meanings of eternal life and death, condemnation, paradise and hell, resurrection and judgement.

Chapter 21 is a continuation of the vision of Chapter 20. In Chapter 21, He who is seated on the throne, who has been identified with God, establishes His reign on earth, insomuch as He comes to dwell on earth, and to be the God of His children.

"Behold, the tabernacle of God is with men, and he will dwell with them, and they shall be his people, and God himself

shall be with them, and be their God."
(Rev. 21:3)

When we discussed the one thousand year reign mentioned in Rev. 20:7, we said that those thousand years did not fulfill the expectations of the Christians for the reign of peace. But we see that the promised Kingdom of God in Chapter 21 does bring universal peace, because we read that the nations will be guided by the light of the city of God:

> "the nations of them which are saved shall walk in the light of it; and the kings of the earth do bring their glory and honour into it." (Rev. 21:24)

What is more, this is the age when human happiness will be widely diffused:

> "And God shall wipe away all tears from their eyes; and there shall be no more death, neither shall there be any more pain...." (Rev. 21:4)

Humanity will be faithful to its God and will fulfill its highest spiritual destiny so long forgotten in wars and suffering:

> "... he will dwell with them, and they shall be his people" (Rev. 21:3)

> "... and his servants shall serve him: And they shall see his face; and his name shall be in their foreheads." (Rev. 22:3-4)

All these things are implied in the words:

> "Behold, I make all things new" (Rev. 21:5)

We should consider that the words "all things" include ALL, including religion and its laws as well. Are we prepared to accept the test

The Millennium; The New Jerusalem

of a great change, even in our religion? In the time of Jesus the Jews were not. They were expecting the Messiah to repeat all of the Mosaic Law, and when Jesus changed the Law, they rebelled against Him. In Revelation Jesus warns us of great new changes. Won't these include changes in the religion, as in His own time?

Therefore, Chapters 21 and 22 are principally dedicated to symbols related to the new religion. With the Dispensation of Bahá'u'lláh which is destined to establish the final stage in the spiritual evolution of man, the Golden Millennium, the author of Revelation has shared with us His most brilliant images to communicate to us a glimpse of the glory which is to come to the world. In particular, it is here where we learn of the marvelous vision of:

"the holy city, new Jerusalem, coming down from God out of heaven..." (Rev. 21:2)

What is the meaning of descending "from God out of heaven"? Some will want to interpret this literally, but careful consideration of the text will show that not to be true. In current terminology, heaven has two meanings:

1. The atmosphere, which constitutes the material heaven.
2. The spiritual world, which is the spiritual heaven.

To what heaven in Revelation referring when it says that the New Jerusalem descends "from

God"? Years ago, people could believe that God lived in the clouds, or in the space among the stars, but today we can all read that which Jesus said: "God is a Spirit" (John 4:24). We recognize that God is invisible and infinite and, being Spirit, His dwelling place is in the spiritual world, far beyond His creation and man. Thus, when Revelation says that the New Jerusalem descends "from God out of heaven", it means that the New Jerusalem comes from the spiritual world and not from the material heaven which is the atmosphere.

We see that the New Jerusalem is compared to a woman, that is, a bride:

"Come hither, I will shew thee the bride, the Lamb's wife. And he showed me that great city, the holy Jerusalem ..." (Rev. 21:9-10)

In Chapter 12 we saw that the woman clothed with the sun represented the Law of God revealed by Muḥammad and in Chapter 11 we interpreted the Holy City as that same law. In the same way, in relation to the New Jerusalem, 'Abdu'l-Bahá says:

"By that great city, the holy Jerusalem, descending out of heaven from God' is meant the holy Law of God"[5]

But we see that this City represents the law revealed by Bahá'u'lláh, since the city comes in the epoch of Him seated on the throne and has "the Glory of God" (Rev. 21:11), in reference to the name of Bahá'u'lláh.

Furthermore, we see that the City-woman has a special relationship with the Lamb (the Báb):

The Millennium; The New Jerusalem

"... the bride, the Lamb's wife ... that great Holy City of Jerusalem" (Rev. 21:9-10)

In Chapter 10 of the present work, "The two prophets of the modern age" we referred to the relationship between the Báb and Bahá'u'lláh, saying that Their Missions and Messages are inseparable. Here again, we see the close relationship between their Dispensations emphasized by the law of Bahá'u'lláh being represented as the wife of the Báb; that is to say, the law that Bahá'u'lláh brought complemented and fulfilled the expectations of the Message of the Báb.

This corresponds to that which we read in the letter to the sixth church, that is, to the followers of the Báb:

"to Him that overcometh... I will write upon him the name of my God, and the name of the city of my God, which is New Jerusalem ..." (Rev. 3:12)

In other words, the new Jerusalem was promised to the Báb and to His followers.

In Revelation 11:2 we read that the Holy City (in that case the Law of God revealed by Muḥammad) was trodden on for forty-two months (1.260 years). The New Jerusalem, the Holy City of Bahá'u'lláh, comes to replace the former Jerusalem which was trodden under. But while the former City was not measured with the rod because (according to Biblical text) it was given to be trodden under foot (Rev. 11:2) the new City is measured entirely (Rev. 21:16).

We infer that now it is not given to be trodden on, but that the New Jerusalem is protected from violation:

> "And there shall in no wise enter into it any thing that defileth, neither whatsoever worketh abomination, or maketh a lie: but they which are written in the Lamb's book of life." (Rev. 21:27)

This shows that the new Law of God will not suffer corruption as in times past. One very special aspect of the new law is the Testament or Covenant of Bahá'u'lláh, through which the unity of the Bahá'í Faith was protected. This same Convenant also protects the purity of the Law of God in that Bahá'u'lláh specified that 'Abdu'l-Bahá was the sole Interpreter of the Bahá'í teachings. 'Abdu'l-Bahá in turn, designated His grandson, Shoghi Effendi as the "expounder of the teachings". The naming of 'Abdu'l-Bahá as Interpreter and Shoghi Effendi as expounder assured a faithful interpretation of the Writings of Bahá'u'lláh, thus avoiding the contradictions of doctrine that have divided the religions of the past. Although any Bahá'í has the right to express his opinions freely about the meanings of the Bahá'í Writings (without contradicting the explicit text), these opinions cannot be construed as representing Bahá'í doctrine, much less be cause to form a separate sect as happened in Islám and Christianity. This is the wisdom of the Covenant of Bahá'u'lláh.

Furthermore, in this new age, each Bahá'í has the privilege and obligation to know and

The Millennium; The New Jerusalem

study the Word of God, according to the principle of independent investigation of truth. Public and universal education in this modern age has made possible the individual study of the Sacred Writings, therefore, in the Bahá'í Faith there is no professional clergy with the responsibility to explain the Holy Word. This may be the meaning of the following passage which mentions the sun and the moon, insomuch as in the Holy Books, the celestial bodies at times refer to the clergy, as we have seen before.

".. the city had no need of the sun, neither of the moon, to shine in it: for the glory of God did lighten it..." (Rev. 21:23)

We note that the name Bahá'u'lláh is included in the previous verse: "because the Glory of God did lighten it". The name of Bahá'u'lláh means the "Glory of God" and the Glory of God gave its light (knowledge and guidance) to the City.

Another reference to the incorruptible nature of the New Jerusalem is the following:

"...and there shall be no more death...."
(Rev. 21:4)

Here death refers to spiritual death, or the lack of consciousness of God and the lack of spirituality. In the past, each religion brought a resurrection, a spiritual rebirth, but with time the spirituality was obscured by superstition and rituals, by self-love and materialism. The promise that "there will be no more death" implies a lasting spirituality that will not suffer corruption as in the past. Likewise, this is the meaning of the following words:

"...and there shall be no more night there." (Rev. 21:25)

That is, this is the day (epoch or Revelation) that will not be followed by darkness.

Upon measuring that Holy City, that is, when we evaluate and study the new Law of God, we see that the number twelve has a special significance. The City has twelve foundations and twelve gates (Rev. (21:12). Concerning this, 'Abdu'l-Bahá comments:

".... the Sun of Truth shineth out from and sheddeth its bounties through twelve stations of holiness, and by these heavenly signs are meant those stainless and unsullied personages who are the very well-springs of sanctity, and the dawning-points proclaiming the oneness of God. Consider how in the days of the Interlocutor (Moses), there were twelve holy beings who were leaders of the twelve tribes; and likewise in the dispensation of the Spirit (Christ), note that there were twelve Apostles gathered within the sheltering shade of that supernal Light, and from those splendid dawning-points the Sun of Truth shone forth even as the sun in the sky. Again, in the days of Muḥammad, observe that there were twelve dawning-points of holiness, the manifestors of God's confirming help. Such is the way of it.

Accordingly did Saint John the Divine tell of twelve gates in his vision, and twelve foundations."[5]

"The meaning of the passage is that this heavenly Jerusalem hath twelve gates, through which the blessed enter into the City of God. These gates are souls who are as guiding stars, as portals of knowledge and grace; and within these gates there stand twelve angels. By 'angel' is meant the power of the confirmations of God — that the candle of God's confirming power shineth out from the lampniche of those souls — meaning that every one of those beings will be granted the most vehement confirming support. These twelve gates surround the entire world, that is they are a shelter for all creatures. And further, these twelve gates are the foundation of the City of God, the heavenly Jerusalem, and on each one of these foundations is written the name of one of the Apostles of Christ. That is to say, each one maketh manifest the perfections, the joyous message, and the excellency of that holy Being."[6]

It is clear, according to these words of 'Abdu'l-Bahá, that the twelve gates are individuals comparable with the Apostles of Christ, who were to guide humanity to the Cause of God, although 'Abdu'l-Bahá did not indicate who these persons were, nor when their identity would be known. In the Bahá'í Faith these appear to be the first Hands of the Cause named by Shoghi Effendi as a group of twelve in 1951, thirty years after the passing of 'Abdu'l-Bahá. Just as Jesus entrusted the teaching of the Evangel to the twelve Disciples, the Hands of the Cause were charged with the special responsibility of propagation and protection of the Cause.

'Abdu'l-Bahá said that these individuals manifest the qualities of the twelve Disciples[7], and that this is the meaning of the names of the twelve Apostles recorded in the foundations of the City. In His own Testament, 'Abdu'l-Bahá speaks of the Disciples of Christ and of the Hands of the Cause in very similar terms. 'Abdu'l-Bahá made the Disciples of Christ an example for the Hands (and for all the Bahá'ís) and in particular, emphasized their qualities of purity and detachment that brought about the transformation of the world. In another passage of His Testament, 'Abdu'l-Bahá again mentions these same qualities in relation to the Hands, saying that they have the "obligation" to "be in every moment and under all conditions, purified and detached from all earthly things"[8]. While every Bahá'í should emulate the Disciples of Christ in his life, only for the Hands was it made an obligation to be always "purified and detached", thus vindicating their position as spiritual sucessors of the Disciples.

Also, these individuals were represented as an integral part of the New Jerusalem, as the very foundation of the same. The Hands of the

The Millennium; The New Jerusalem

Cause, more than dedicated teachers, constitute an indispensable part of the Bahá'í Administration. In language reminiscent of Revelation, Shoghi Effendi said that the naming of the twelve Hands marked a very significant step that prepared the way to "STRENGTHEN FOUNDATIONS BAHÁ'Í ADMINISTRATIVE ORDER"[9], that it would lead eventually to the election of the Universal House of Justice which is the supreme institution of the New Jerusalem (Law of God). Shoghi Effendi said in a cable of the Bahá'í world:

INITIAL STEP NOW TAKEN (of naming the Hands of the Cause) REGARDED PREPARATORY FULL DEVELOPMENT INSTITUTION PROVIDED 'ABDU'L-BAHÁ'S WILL, PARALLELED PRELIMINARY MEASURE FORMATION INTERNATIONAL COUNCIL DESTINED CULMINATE EMERGENCE UNIVERSAL HOUSE OF JUSTICE.

Eventually, the body of the Hands of the Cause grew to twenty-seven and they were in a large part responsible, after the passing of Shoghi Effendi in 1957, for the election of the Universal House of Justice, thus fulfilling the expectations of the Guardian.

But in the first contingent there were named only twelve Hands of the Cause, in groups of three for each of four specific areas: Irán, Europe, Israel, and the Americas, respectively. Revelation refers to the geographical distribution of the Hands of the Cause when it says that the city has:

"On the east, three gates; on the north, three gates; on the south, three gates, and on the west, three gates." (Rev. 21:13)

We also see that the tree of life in the New Jerusalem yields twelve kinds of fruits. We can interpret the twelve fruits as symbolic of the twelve basic teachings of the new religion; fruits by which Jesus said that one could distinguish the true Prophet from the false: "By their fruits ye shall know them".

These twelve basic principles are summarized by 'Abdu'l-Bahá[11]. They are as follows:

1. Independent investigation of truth: God has granted to each human being an intelligence, with which the individual should search the sacred books to discover the truth, free from prejudices and with open mind. More than a declaration of intellectual freedom, this is an obligation of each individual, insomuch as the faith of no person can be conditioned by another.
2. The essential harmony of science and religion: reality is one, not one scientific and the other spiritual. If there existed conflict in the past between theologians and scientists, it was due in large part to superstitions introduced into religion. Religion without science becomes superstition, while science without the moral guidance of religion can destroy humanity. Science and religon are the two

most powerful forces for the advancement of civilization, when they function together.
3. Religion should be the cause of love and harmony: God has revealed religions to create unity among men. If religion becomes the cause of hatred, division, and wars, it is better that it not exist.
4. The oneness of mankind: There is only one God Who has created all mankind. We are all His children, and all benefit from His blessings. All derive our existence from the same Source, therefore, the unity of mankind is a fact of our existence, and not a utopian ideal.
5. Universal Peace: The cause of universal peace urgently requires the establishment of a Supreme Tribunal with authority to judge in cases of conflict between nations, thus avoiding armed confrontations.
6. One universal language: Bahá'u'lláh says that the governments of the wrold should choose a universal auxiliary language to be taught in all of the schools of the world in addition to the mother language of each country. A universal language will facilitate the communication between peoples and governments, will serve in international commerce, will increase mutual understanding, and will be a powerful force to establish peace. Such language can be one of those existing already or can be one invented especially for this purpose.

7. Universal education: We were all created by God with talents and capacities, but an adequate education is necessary to develop these talents. While every child, male or female, should be educated equally if possible, it is especially urgent to educate the young women for they will become the mothers of the next generation, and the mother is the first educator of every human being. With the education of mothers, a whole generation is educated.
8. Equality of men and women: Spiritually there is no difference between men and women, and intellectually they have the same capacities. It is widely demonstrated that women are capable of fulfilling any profession, but the lack of opportunities has denied them an equal position with men. The discrimination against women, which begins in the home itself, is an especially noxious custom, an injustice against one half of the world's population; this discrimination is harmful even to men, creating in them attitudes of superiority and aggressiveness which have a negative effect in every relationship, including the relations between governments.
9. Universal Justice: Human beings have the right to equality before the law.
10. Work for all: We all have the right to a means of existence, and equality of opportunity should exist, beginning with education. It is not just that a few live in

riches, and others wander in the streets, begging for whatever opportunity to work and sustain themselves, albeit inadequately.

11. Elimination of all classes of prejudice and elimination of the extremes of poverty and wealth: Prejudices of whatever kind, whether of race, sex, religion or social class, are contrary to the principle of unity of mankind, and should be eliminated by means of education. These prejudices have divided humanity and have led men to war, the same as have the extremes of wealth and poverty, which many times are an economic expression of some type of prejudice. Although economic equality is impossible, in the future mankind will not accept the economic extremes that prevail today.

12. The Holy Spirit should be the propelling force of life: Every effort to improve human life will be a failure without a firm spiritual base. From his faith in God, man derives his will to change and an impartial desire to serve his kind. But far from being a limited faith of religious rites, this faith should be natural and spontaneous reaction that springs from the heart which has recognized its Lord. Once this faith is engendered, men should seek guidance from the Holy Spirit, both in moments of prayer and reflection as in the inspired words of the Prophets.

The Writings of Bahá'u'lláh, 'Abdu'l-Bahá, and Shoghi Effendi reveal these and other principles in more detail, but in relation to the Apocalyptic theme of Universal Peace, it is appropriate to explore more deeply the Bahá'í teachings which will serve humanity on its path from the present turmoil to a future of peace, from "its Calvary to its resurrection". In particular, Bahá'u'lláh declares as an indispensable step to obtain peace, that the rulers of the world unite in a Universal Assemblage specifically to establish peace:

"The time must come when the imperative necessity for the holding of a vast, an all-embracing assemblage of men will be universally realized. The rulers and kings of the earth must needs attend it, and, participating in its deliberations, must consider such ways and means as will lay the foundations of the world's Great Peace amongst men."[12]

'Abdu'l-Bahá, commenting on the deliberations that must take place in this Universal Assemblage, says:

"They must make the Cause of Peace the object of general consultation, and seek by every means in their power to establish a Union of the nations of the world. They must conclude a binding treaty and establish a covenant, the provisions of which shall be sound, inviolable and definite. They must proclaim it to all the world and obtain for it the sanction of all the human race. This supreme and noble undertaking — the real

The Millennium; The New Jerusalem

source of the peace and well-being of all the world—should be regarded as sacred by all that dwell on earth. All the forces of humanity must be mobilized to ensure the stability and permanence of this Most Great Covenant. In this all-embracing Pact the limits and frontiers of each and every nation should be clearly fixed, the principles underlying the relations of governments towards one another definitely laid down, and all international agreements and obligations ascertained. In like manner, the size of the armaments of every government should be strictly limited, for if the preparations for war and the military forces of any nation should be allowed to increase, they will arouse the suspicion of others. The fundamental principle underlying this solemn Pact should be so fixed that if any government later violate any one of its provisions, all the governments on earth should arise to reduce it to utter submission, nay the human race as a whole should resolve, with every power at its disposal, to destroy that government. Should this greatest of all remedies be applied to the sick body of the world, it will assuredly recover from its ills and will remain eternally safe and secure."[13]

The "relations between governments" to which 'Abdu'l-Bahá refers should be defined in a way that the national governments establish a world government in which the national governments participate as members of a federal state:

> "Some form of a world super-state must needs be evolved, in whose favour all the nations of the world will have willingly ceded every claim to make war, certain rights to impose taxation and all rights to maintain armaments, except for purposes of maintaining internal order within their respective dominions. Such a state will have to include within its orbit an International Executive adequate to enforce supreme and unchallengeable authority on every recalcitrant member of the commonwealth; a World Parliament whose members shall be elected by the people in their respective countries and whose election shall be confirmed by their respective governments; and a Supreme Tribunal whose judgement will have a binding effect even in such cases where the parties concerned did not voluntarily agree to submit their case to its consideration."[14]

Such world government, far from being cause of new oppressions, will be the instrument to establish a world civilization which must reflect the high precepts which Bahá'u'lláh espoused:

> "...the city had no need of the sun, neither of the moon, to shine in it: for the glory of God did lighten it, and the Lamb is the light thereof. And the nations of them which are saved shall walk in the light of

it: and the kings of the earth do bring their glory and honour into it." (Rev. 21:23-24)

Since the purpose of these verses of Revelation is to open our eyes to the glorious future which awaits us, it is appropriate to end this chapter with some words of Shoghi Effendi about the Golden Millennium and the characteristics of this civilization destined to be born from the matrix of the Message of Bahá'u'lláh. Shoghi Effendi says:

"A world metropolis will act as the nerve centre of a world civilization, the focus towards which the unifying forces of life will converge and from which its energizing influences will radiate. A world language will either be invented or chosen from among the existing languages and will be taught in the schools of all the federated nations as an auxiliary to their mother tongue. A world script, a world literature, a uniform and universal system of currency, of weights and measures, will simplify and facilitate intercourse and understanding among the nations and races of mankind. In such a world society, science and religion, the two most potent forces in human life, will be reconciled, will cooperate, and will harmoniously develop. The press will, under such a system, while giving full scope to the expression of the diversified views and convictions of mankind, cease to be mischievously manipulated by vested interests, whether private or public, and will be liberated from the influence of contending governments and poeples. The economic resources of the world will be organized, its sources of raw materials will be tapped and fully utilized, its markets will be coordinated and developed, and the distribution of its products will be equitably regulated. National rivalries, hatreds, and intrigues will cease, and racial animosity and prejudice will be replaced by racial amity, understanding and cooperation. The causes of religious strife will be permanently removed, economic barriers and restrictions will be completely abolished, and the inordinate distinction between classes will be obliterated. Destitution on the one hand, and gross accumulation of ownership on the other, will disappear. The enormous energy dissipated and wasted on war, whether economic or political, will be consecrated to such ends as will extend the range of human inventions and technical development, to the increase of the productivity of mankind, to the extermination of disease, to the extension of scientific research, to the raising of the standard of physical health, to the sharpening and refinement of the human brain, to the exploitation of the unused and unsuspected resources of the planet, to the prolongation of human life, and to the furtherance of any other agency that can stimulate the intellectual, the moral, and spiritual life of the entire human race.[15]

REFERENCES

1. W.E. Blackstone, *Jesus Comes*, p. 24.
2. Shoghi Effendi, *God Passes By*, p. 58.
3. Bahá'u'lláh, *Book of Certitude*, p. 199.
4. Shoghi Effendi, *God Passes By*, p. 139.
5. 'Abdu'l-Bahá, *Selections from the Writings of 'Abdu'l-Bahá*, p. 165, ⁻142.
6. Ibid.
7. See Chapter 9 of this book and Chapter XXXIII of *Some Answered Questions* for a discussion of the subject of the return.
8. 'Abdu'l-Bahá, *Will and Testament*, p. 13.
9. Universal House of Justice, *Bahá'í World* p. 333.
10. Ibid.
11. Shoghi Effendi, *God Passes By*, p. IX of Introduction.
12. Bahá'u'lláh, quoted in, Universal House of Justice, *The Promise of World Peace*, p. 19-20.
13. 'Abdu-l-Bahá, quoted in, Universal House of Justice, *The Promise of World Peace*, p. 20-21.
14. Shoghi Effendi, quoted in, Universal House of Justice, *The Promise of World Peace*, p. 18-19.
15. Shoghi Effendi, *Call to the Nations*, p. 54-56.

CHAPTER 15

Chapter 13: The Two Beasts

No discussion of Revelation would be complete without mentioning Chapter 13, origin of the number 666. This chapter tells the story of the succession of two beasts, one of which receives its sovereignty from the other. Since their power lasts for a period of 42 months, these beasts also pertain to the succession of the illegitimate authority which opposed the descendants of Muḥammad.

Some Bahá'ís have interpreted this chapter in terms of the succession of the Umayyad Dynasty (the first beast) by that of the Abbasid (the second beast). We see that the second beast has all the characteristics which identify it with the Umayyad: seven heads and ten horns. According to this interpretation we would say that the Abbasid Caliphs were the image of the Umayyad, from whom they inherited their illegitimate authority.

Mrs. Ruth Moffet, author of *New Keys to the Book of Revelation,* offers an alternative interpretation based on a conversation with Shoghi Effendi[1]. This explanation seems to reflect very well the historic events of the period of the

Chapter 13: The Two Beasts

Umayyad. According to Mrs. Moffet, the first beast represents Mu'awiyah I, son of Abu-Sufyan, and first Caliph of the Umayyad. It was Mu'awiyah who established a dynasty of the Umayyad in opposition to the Imáms, by means of assassinations and deception.

Mu'awiyah rebelled against the authority of 'Alí, the first Imám of the Shi'ahs with the hope of seizing the Caliphate. This was the start of a civil was between the forces of 'Alí, Mu'awiyah, and yet another usurper, 'Amr. But according to the story, a group of religious fanatics, convinced that 'Alí, as well as Mu'awiyah and 'Amr, were guilty of ambition, decided to kill all three in order to assure peace. As a result of the conspiracy, only 'Alí died. Mu'awiyah suffered injury in the attempt but recovered:

"And I saw one of his heads as it were wounded to death; and his deadly wound was healed..." (Rev. 13:3)

After the death of 'Alí, Mu'awiyah forced a treaty with Ḥasan, 'Alí's son and successor. Ḥasan signed an agreement recognizing Mu'awiyah as Caliph until his death, and then the Caliphate would return to Ḥasan. But Mu'awiyah was unfaithful to his word and designated his son, Yazid, as the next Caliph. Yazid is the second beast which received his sovereignty from the first:

"and the dragon gave him his power, and
his seat, and great authority." (Rev. 13:1)

Ḥasan was poisoned (supposedly at the order of Mu'awiyah) and his brother, Ḥusayn, arose to defend the authority of the Imáms, now violated again with the designation of Yazid as Caliph. This Ḥusayn is the third Imám of whom we have spoken, who died on the plain of Karbila near the Euphrates River. Yazid dispatched an army of four thousand men to confront Ḥusayn and some seventy companions in battle. Ḥusayn and all his companions died heroicly:

> "And it was given unto him to make war with the saints, and to overcome them" (Rev. 13:7).

Later, the inhabitants of Medina rebelled against the corruption of Yazid and he sent an army from Damascus to destroy them. First, Medina was sacked and afterward the army turned toward Mecca to set siege to it also. In this campaign even the Sanctuary of Muḥammad in Medina and the holy Kaaba (temple) in Mecca were damaged. Revelation refers to this upon saying that the tabernacle of God was blasphemed.

> "And he opened his mouth in blasphemy against God, to blaspheme his name, and his tabernacle, and them that dwell in heaven."

As for the number 666, Mrs. Moffet considers that this refers to the year of the Christian Era which is related to the reign of Mu'awiyah, the first beast.

> "Let him that hath understanding count the number of the beast: for it is the number of a man; and his number is six hundred three score and six." (Rev. 13:18)

Chapter 13: The Two Beasts

We don't have many details about the reign of Mu'awiyyah, but we know that it lasted from 661 to 680 A.D. Where does the year 666 figure in the fulfillment of the prophecy? In this respect another Bahá'í author, Mr. Riggs, offers an explanation that is novel and interesting[2]. Mr. Riggs notes that many Christian historians now discount the popular belief that Jesus was born in the year 1 A.D., rather, they believe that he was born some years before. In Mat. 2 we read that Jesus was born during the reign of Herod and Herod died in 4 B.C. according to historical sources. If we assume (according to the belief of some historians) that Jesus was born around the year 5 B.C. and that this marks the true beginning of the Christian Era, then 661 A.D. (year in which Mu'awiyah rose to power) corresponds to the year 666 of the Christian Era. That is to say, "the number of the beast that is the number of a man" is the number of the year that this man-beast committed his great blasphemy against God, declaring himself Caliph and representative of God on earth.

REFERENCES

1. Ruth Moffet, *New Keys to the book of Revelation*, p. 74-80.
2. Robert Riggs, *The Apocalypse Unsealed*, pp. 169-170.

CHAPTER 16

Chapter 14:
The Harvest of the Vineyard

In Chapter 14 of Revelation we also find seven personages and these appear to be the seven Prophets which we have already identified. In particular, we see a certain relationship when we compare Chapter 14 with the seven trumpets of Chapters 8 to 11. However, in chapter 14 we do not find the sequence of the Prophets in seven clearly defined stages; rather, there is overlap between one stage and another.

The first personage of Chapter 14 is an angel who has an "Eternal Evangel" (Rev. 14:6). We would suppose that this is Adam, but there is no particular evidence of this.

In Chapter 8, when the second trumpet sounds, we see that the sea turns to blood. 'Abdu'l-Bahá has explained that the transformation of water into blood means that which before was the cause of life and well-being becomes a cause of spiritual death. In the case of Pharaoh and Moses, the riches and power of Pharaoh were the cause of his honor and high position and are compared with water. But these also made him proud and led him to oppose to Moses and therefore caused his

Chapter 14: The Harvest of the Vineyard

downfall. The attachment to the material world and its passing honors caused the eternal disgrace of Pharaoh.

Turning to Chapter 14, when the second angel appears, he announces the fall of Babylon "because she has made all nations drink of the wine of the wrath of her fornication" (Rev. 14:8). Thus we see that the symbol of blood (Rev. 8:8) has been replaced by the symbol of wine. Again, this wine is the cause of spiritual death of men. In this case "fornication" does not refer necessarily to the sexual act, but an attachment to the material things, the love of the material world, and entanglement of the soul in worldly desires.

When the third trumpet sounded in Chapter 8, the rivers and fountains were contaminated, "and many men died because of the waters, because they were made bitter" (Rev. 8:11). This event has the same significance as the transformation of water into blood. We see a relationship between this and that which the third angel announces in Chapter 14:

> "If any man worship the beast and his image, and receive his mark in his forehead, or in his hand, the same shall drink of the wine of the wrath of God..." (Rev. 14:9-10)

Again, men will die of a fatal draught.

We have related this third stage with Moses, and again we find a relationship between the announcement of the third angel in Revelation 14 and the Old Testament stories. The worship of the beast mentioned in Rev. 14:9 above reminds us of the sin of the Israelites in worshipping the golden calf in the days of Moses.

The fourth Holy Being of Chapter 14 is described as one "like unto the Son of Man" (Rev. 14:14). This Holy Being comes with a sickle and, responding to the call of the fifth Angel, he thrusts in His sickle and reaps the earth. This could well be Jesus, because in the Evangels Jesus said to His disciples that the time of the harvest had come (John 4:35).

The last two angels come almost simultaneously and one also has a sickle. The other encourages Him to harvest the vineyards of the earth and the first harvests the fruit of the vine with His sickle. These are Bahá'u'lláh and the Báb and Bahá'u'lláh is the angel that harvests the vineyards.

The warning for the time of the harvest of the vineyard is threatening:

> "And the angel thrust in his sickle into the earth, and gathered the vine of the earth, and cast it into the great winepress of the wrath of God. And the winepress was trodden without the city, and blood came out of the winepress, even unto the horse bridles, by the space of a thousand and six hundred furlongs." (Rev. 14:19-20)

It is interesting to note how often in prophecy the vineyard is related with the time of judgement. We see one case here in Rev. 14:19. We see another in the parable of the vineyard, where Jesus made the following

Chapter 14: The Harvest of the Vineyard

prophecy of the evil husbandmen of the vineyard:

"What therefore shall the lord of the vineyard do unto them? He shall come and destroy these husbandmen and shall give the vineyard to others." (Luke 20:15-16)

It is important to note also that the name of Mount Carmel, sacred mountain of Israel, means "Vineyard of God", and Mount Carmel figures prominently in the prophecies of the time of the end. Isaiah and Micah mention it as the site of the Manifestation of the One sent from God in the last days, and for centuries the Christians have waited for Jesus to appear there. In the 19th century, a German religious order, the Templars, settled on Mount Carmel to await the return of Christ.

This suggests to us a relationship between the prophecies about Mount Carmel and the parable of the vineyard. The Lord of the vineyard (Mount Carmel) is the Promised One of Isaiah and Micah and is Bahá'u'lláh. In the past century when the authorities permitted Bahá'u'lláh to leave the prison of Akká and to travel locally, He visited Mount Carmel and established it as the Seat of the Universal House of Justice, supreme body of the Bahá'í Faith. "And (He) shall give the vineyard to others". Today the Sanctuaries and administrative buildings of the Bahá'ís occupy a prominent place on the slopes of Carmel, a testimony to the fulfillment of the parable of Jesus and the ancient prophecies.

CHAPTER 17

The Throne of God; The Lamb and the 144,000

What can we say about the significance of the "throne of God"? Is this symbolic of a world of God that is completely beyond our comprehension or does it represent something in this earthly world below?

In a very significant Tablet, the Tablet of Carmel, Bahá'u'lláh established the holy mountain as the seat of the Universal House of Justice (elected in 1963) and promised a glorious future for Mount Carmel. Directing Himself to Mount Carmel in allegorical language, Bahá'u'lláh says:

"Render thanks unto Thy Lord, O Carmel. The fire of thy separation from Me was fast consuming thee, when the ocean of My presence surged before thy face, cheering thine eyes and those of all creation, and filling with delight all things visible and invisible. Rejoice, for God hath in this Day established upon thee His throne, hath made thee the dawning-place of His signs and the day spring of the evidences of His Revelation."[1]

The Throne of God

By these words we understand that Mount Carmel has been designated as the "throne of God" in this world. What other mysteries will be revealed to us by applying this knowledge to the verses of Revelation?

We read of the throne that:

"there was a rainbow round about the throne, in sight like unto an emerald" (Rev. 4:3).

This has at least two meanings. In the story of Noah, the rainbow was a symbol of the Covenant between God and His children. The rainbow around the throne implies a renewal of this Covenant in the last days and a relationship of the New Covenant with the throne, on Mount Carmel.

However, this rainbow is not like any other, in that it is green like an "emerald". What does this mean? Upon Mount Carmel one finds an arc (that is to say, a path traced in a curve) on which is situated the Seat of the Universal House of Justice. This arc sketched on the slopes is surrounded by beautiful gardens of luminous green, "in appearance like unto an emerald", in contrast with the mountain around it, where wild vegetation grows among the stones.

We see in several verses that the Lamb (the Báb) is in the vicinity of the throne (Mount Carmel):

"And I beheld, and, lo, in the midst of the throne and of the four living beings and in the midst of the elders, stood a Lamb." (Rev. 5:6)

"For the Lamb which is in the midst of the throne shall feed them" (Rev. 7:17)

This is true in fact, because we know that the remains of the Báb repose in a Sanctuary in the midst of Carmel. Thus it appears that these verses refer to the Sanctuary of the Báb on Mount Carmel.

Furthermore, we also see that the Lamb is in the vicinity of the 144,000 who were chosen of God:

"And I looked, and lo, a Lamb stood on the Mount Sion and with him one hundred forty four thousand." (Rev. 14:1)

The identity of the 144,000 is one of the most hotly discussed topics of Revelation insomuch as everyone aspires to be counted amongst them. Before making an attempt to decipher their identity, it is easier to indicate first who they are NOT.

The election of the 144,000 is described as the gathering of the twelve tribes of Israel and bears a certain likeness to the prophecies of the return of the Jews to the Holy Land in the last days. However, the election of the 144,000 is evidently symbolic and not necessarily connected to the modern exodus, because its literal fulfillment is impossible. The primitive structure of the Israelite society, that is, the tribes of Israel, disappeared with the dispersion of the Jews into the nations of the world. Even in the time of Jesus, the ten tribes of the Northern Kingdom had suffered a disastrous dispersion and to this day the fate of the tribes of the

North is a mystery. From this we conclude that the 144,000 chosen ones of the twelve tribes of Israel do not represent literally the reuniting of the Israelites in the last days. What is more, this interpretation wouldn't be in accord with recent historical facts either, since many more Jews have returned to Israel than the 144,000 mentioned in Revelation.

Furthermore, it is curious that the twelve tribes named in Revelation 7, are incorrectly identified with respect to the twelve ancient tribes of Israel. In Revelation 7:7 there is mentioned the tribe of Levi, although the descendants of Levi were priests and normally are not identified as a separate tribe. Moreover, there is no mention of the tribe of Dan and there is one of Joseph, although in the twelve ancient tribes Joseph was represented in the twelve tribes through his sons, Ephraim and Manasseh, and there is usually no mention of a tribe of Joseph *per se*. Neither was the tribe of Ephraim named in Revelation. The inexact identification of the twelve tribes emphasizes their symbolic nature.

Neither do the 144,000 represent the only souls to be saved in the last days, in contrast to that which some believe, for in the same chapter where we are acquainted with the 144,000, we also read of a multitude without number:

"... a great multitude, which no man could number, of all nations, and kindreds, and peoples, and tongues, stood before the throne, ... These are they which came out of great tribulation, and have washed their robes, and made them white in the blood of the Lamb." (Rev. 7:9-14)

On the contrary to there being a strictly limited number of souls among the saved, here the saved are represented as "a great multitude, which no man could number". It is obvious that God has not put a limit on the number of souls that can attain paradise. Rather, the prophecies of Revelation and of the Old Testament present to us a vision of a salvation ever wider, that includes "all nations and kindreds and people and tongues".

These observations indicate to us who the 144,000 are NOT. But what can we learn about the 144,000 that will help us to decipher their true identity? First, we see that the 144,000 are associated with Mount Zion:

"And I looked, and lo, a Lamb stood on the Mount Sion, and with him one hundred forty and four thousand..." (Rev. 14:1)

We read in the Book of Isaiah that "The Lord hath founded Zion" (Is. 14:32), suggesting that Zion is symbolic of something more than a physical mountain. In the Old Testament, Zion is used alternately with the name of Jerusalem, which we already have seen is a symbol of the Law of God. Moreover, in the prophecies of the last days, Zion is identified as the source of the New Law:

"And it shall come to pass in the last days, that the mountain of the Lord's house shall be established in the top of the mountains, and shall be exalted above the hills; and all nations shall flow unto it. And many people shall go and say, Come ye, and let us go up to the mountain of the Lord, to the house of the God of Jacob; and he will teach us of his ways, and we will walk in his paths: for out of Zion shall go forth the law ..." (Isaiah 2:2-3)

These verses suggest a symbolic meaning of Zion closely linked with the law that is to come in the last days and from the proximity of the 144,000 to Zion, we infer that they also are related in some form with this law.

The restoration of the twelve tribes of Israel implies another relationship with the law, since these tribes have not existed as such since approximately 800 B.C., when Assyria destroyed the Northern Kingdom. The restoration implies a return, in some sense, to the time of Moses, Joshua, and the Judges, when the twelve tribes existed. This was a time of theocracy, that is, a society whose law was the divine law. Such a restoration of a just government and with a divine foundation was promised by Isaiah:

> "And I will restore thy judges as at the first, and thy counsellors as at the beginning; afterward thou shalt be called, The city of righteousness, the faithful city." (Is. 1:26)

It is significant that we find in the Bible two descriptions of the destiny of the twelve tribes in the last days. One is here in Revelation 17 and the other we find in the first pages of the Old

Testament, in Genesis 49. It is the last blessing of Jacob for his twelve sons before he died, when he tells them:

> "Gather yourselves together and I will tell you that which shall befall you in the last days." (Gen. 49:1)

The sons of Jacob were the founders of the twelve tribes and gave their names to the tribes with the exception of Joseph and Levi, as we have already explained.

We have said that the assemblage of the twelve tribes of Revelation must be symbolic, in that these no longer exist in our times. For the same reason, the words of Jacob must be symbolic also, and it is reasonable to suggest that the twelve tribes have a similar symbolic reality in Genesis and in Revelation.

In the Qurán also, it is stated that the story of Jacob and his sons is "the most beautiful of the stories revealed in the Qurán"[2], and that "in Joseph and his brothers are proofs ... for those who look"[3].

Then what clues do we find in the words of Jacob in Genesis that can reveal the identity of the twelve tribes in our days? To facilitate the study, in Table 3 is found a summary of the prophecies which Jacob made for his sons and also the meaning of each son's name, which in many cases is related to the prophecy. For example, the name "Dan" means "to judge" and the prophecy says "Dan will judge his people" (Gen. 49:16).

We see that the promises of Jacob for his twelve sons are not all the same. Jacob predicts a glorious future for some (Judah and Joseph) while he strongly condemns others (Simeon, Levi, and Benjamin). We will find the promise to Judah of particular interest:

> "Judah, thou art he whom thy brethren shall praise; thy hand shall be on the neck of thine enemies, thy father's children shall bow down before thee. Judah is a lion's whelp; from the prey, my son, thou art gone up: he stooped down, he couched as a lion, and as an old lion. Who shall rouse him up? The sceptre shall not depart from Judah, nor a lawgiver from between his feet, until Shiloh come; and unto him shall the gathering of the people be." (Gen. 49:8-10)

There are several clear signs here that relate Judah with the Messiah and the religion of the last days. These signs are as follows:
1. Judah is compared with a lion. We find another reference to this in Revelation 5:5 where the Messiah is identified as the "Lion of the tribe of Judah".
2. The sceptre and "the lawgiver" pertain to Judah, that is, the government of the earth in the last days.
3. Judah also gathers the peoples together. This may refer to the reuniting of the Jews in the last days, or to the unification of all the peoples of the earth, but in either case, it applies to the Messiah of the last days. We have stated that this Messiah is Bahá'u'lláh[4] who came to

establish a universal system of government and to unify the peoples of the earth.

TABLE 3
Sons of Jacob, Meanings of their Names, and Prophecies of Jacob for his Descendants (Genesis 49)

Name	Meaning	Blessing and Prophecies of Jacob for the Last Days
1. Reuben	Behold a son	First born, might, dignity, strength of Jacob; condemned for usurping father's rights.
2. Simeon	A hearkening	Simeon and Levi conspired together to kill a man;
3. Levi	Associate	For their crime they were scattered.
4. Judah	Praised	Compared to a Lion; will conquer his enemies; the sceptre of legislation will be his; he will gather together the people.
5. Zebulun	Abode	Will live by the sea; will be a port for ships.
6. Issachar	He is hired	Like an ass resting from his burdens, he served tribute.
7. Dan	Judge	Shall judge his people; like a serpent on the road.
8. Gad	Good fortune	Will be conquered by an army, but in the end he will conquer.
9. Asher	Fortunate	His bread will be fat and will give dainties to kings.
10. Naphtali	My Fight	A hind let loose.
11. Joseph	He shall add	A fruitful bough; attacked by archers; will conquer his enemies in the end; will be bountifully blessed by God.
12. Benjamin	Son of the right hand	A devouring wolf.

Another prophecy of Jacob for his sons seems to be related with the Jews and the crucifixion of Christ. Jacob says:
"Simeon and Levi are brethren; instruments of cruelty are in their habitations. O my soul, come not thou into their secret; unto their assembly, mine honour, be not thou united: for in their anger they slew a man, and in their self will they digged down a wall. Cursed by their anger, for it was fierce; and their wrath, for it was cruel: I will divide them in Jacob, and scatter them in Israel." (Gen. 49:5-7)

In so much as this prophecy speaks of the scattering of the Israelites, apparently it is in reference to the exiles which the Israelites suffered. In particular, this exile is a punishment for having killed a man, that is, for having crucified Christ. It is significant that this judgement is directed to Levi, in that years later the Levites were the priests of the Jews and those same priests (among them Caiaphas) condemned and crucified Christ.

We would suppose that the descendants of the other brothers also would be an object of this judgement, but we have already seen that Judah was promised a glorious future. It appears that Simeon and Levi were chosen as representative of all the Israelites in the coming years, that is they represent the Jewish religion in the days of Jesus and afterwards, during the long period of the dispersion which only ended in this modern age.

With these two examples, we begin to see a pattern: Levi and Simeon represent the Jewish religion in the days of Christ and afterwards. Judah represents the Messiah and the religion of the latter days. Thus, we see that the descendants of the sons of Jacob, the twelve tribes, represent the religions which God has sent to the world through His Messengers and in particular (according to the words of Jacob) the prophecies speak of the destiny of the destiny of these religions in the latter days.

If we follow this line of investigation, we can discover possible symbolic identities of the other twelve sons of Jacob.

Reuben is described as the "first born" who was the image of his father, manifesting "strength", "might", "dignity" and "power". These remind us of Adám, who was the first created by God (His "first born") and made in the image of God. Moreover, Adám fell in disgrace because he ate of the forbidden tree, aspiring to make himself equal to God in knowledge. Reuben is also condemned for usurping that which belonged to his father.

The destinies of Gad and Joseph are very similar, in that the two were attacked by armies but later conquered their enemies. These represent the Báb[5] and the Imám Husayn respectively, who were martyred by armies in different ages, but whose Causes later overcame these tribulations. Of Gad we read that "a troop shall overcome him: but he shall overcome at last" (Gen 49:19). Thus was the Báb martyred by a regiment of 750 soldiers, but His Cause survived to encircle the globe. The prophecy says that the archers "caused grief" to Joseph, such as occurred in the case of Ḥusayn, who saw his infant son die in his arms, victim of an enemy arrow. The Báb Himself has drawn a relationship between Joseph and Ḥusayn[6], and we see certain similarities between the two, in that each was the most illustrious among a group of twelve, destined to suffer great pain and tribulation.

Of Asher it is said that "his bread shall be fat". The significance of this promise may be related to the geography of the ancient tribes. When to each tribe a certain region of Palestine was assigned, the tribe of Asher received the region where today the city of Akká is located, city where Bahá'u'lláh was imprisoned for many years and where His long exiles ended. To say that the bread of Asher will be "fat", implies abundance - which is to say, spiritual abundance. For it was in Akká that Bahá'u'lláh revealed some of His most significant works, most notably the Kitáb-i-Aqdas, containing the laws and ordinances for the modern age. In another sense, "fat bread" suggests the end of a journey. When the Hebrews abandoned Egypt under the leadership of Moses and initiated their forty years of wandering, they did so in such haste that they did not have time to leaven their bread. In later years unleavened bread would be a symbol of their hurried departure. "Fat" or well-leavened bread, on the other hand, denotes the end of a journey, rest and stability. Indeed, it was in the land of Asher where Bahá'u'lláh ended His exiles (forty years worth!), and where eventually He found peace and tranquility.

Zebulun "shall dwell at the haven of the sea". When applied to the latter days, this blessing also appears to be associated with the geography of the twelve tribes. The region that pertained to Zebulun was that by the sea around modern-day Haifa and Mount Carmel. In the study of the seven stages of Revelation, we associated the sea with the Prophet Noah. The name Zebulun means "dwelling" and the name Noah means "rest", both suggestive of protection such as the believers found within the ark. Assuming that Zabulun represents Noah, we see in the prophecy of Jacob that in the latter days the Cause of Noah (or His Covenant) would be associated with the land of Zebulun, that is, with Haifa and Carmel. In the present chapter we also noted the rainbow of the Covenant (a symbol of the Covenant from the days of Noah) surrounds the throne of God (Carmel). Alluding to His own Covenant in the symbolism of Noah's Ark, in the Tablet of Carmel Bahá'u'lláh addresses the Holy Mountain saying, "Ere long will God sail His Ark upon thee..." For just as in ancient times the Ark of Noah came to rest on the slopes of Mount Ararat, so did the Ark (Covenant) of Bahá'u'lláh come to rest on Mount Carmel!

Zebulun will be a "haven for ships". In a material sense, Haifa is today the principal

The Throne of God

seaport of modern Israel, a fact that has been fully realized only in this century, for until the nineteenth century Haifa was little more than a small fishing village. Spiritually speaking, Haifa is a "haven" for the peoples of the world, insomuch as it is the world center of the Bahá'í Faith where the Seat of the Universal House of Justice is located.

Of Benjamin it is said that he will "ravin as a wolf", description which could well apply to many in the present age. Perhaps the only clue to his prophetic identity is in his name. When Benjamin was born, his mother Rachel named him "Ben-oni" (son of my sorrow), but Jacob called him "Benjamin" (son of the right hand). Both names and especially "Son of the right hand", suggest a relationship with Jesus Christ, who spoke of being seated at the right hand of His Father. If this is the case, the prophecy of Jacob would not refer to the true Cause of Jesus, of course, but to the tragic condition of Christianity after two thousand years. Would the condemnation of Benjamin be a judgement of our Western civilization, Christian in name but source of the greatest evils that harass humanity? Examples of such evils are the two most destructive wars in the history of the world which pitted Christian against Christian; a colonial system which submitted entire continents to its dominon; and ironically, a materialistc philosophy formulated as a science, that denies the very existence of God.

The prophecies directed to the other brothers are possibly in reference to the Hebrews in various periods of their history. For example, Dan will "judge his people" and of him Jacob exclaims "I have waited for thy salvation, Oh Lord". A judgement implies a law and it was Moses who brought the law and for whom the Hebrews waited during their long captivity in Egypt to save them from their misery. Also, Dan is as a "serpent by the way", and the serpent was one of the symbols of the authority of Moses.

Issachar becomes a "servant of tribute", such as the Jews in later years, under the dominion of the Assyrians, Babylonians, Persians, Greeks, and Romans successively.

Considered as a whole, the twelve tribes represent the history of religion over the last six thousand years, from Adám (Reuben) to Bahá'u'lláh (Judah). We see that this is the same interpretation which we gave to the seven churches of Revelation. Both Jacob and the author of Revelation have used the believers of their own respective periods to symbolize a process that has spanned six thousand years.

This is a theme that requires much careful reflection to appreciate fully and to understand its significance when we return to Revelation and consider again the prophecy of the twelve tribes of Israel.

This process of six thousand years which we have called "progressive revelation" represents the spiritual evolution of humanity. Just as the world has experienced social and intellectual progress, its spiritual life also displays an

The Throne of God

evolution and a tendency to ascend, considering this from the dawn of history until the present. Thus, the twelve tribes represent the various stages through which humanity has passed in its spiritual odyssey.

The foundation of Progressive Revelation is the Eternal Covenant of God, the supreme principle that governs the relationship between God and man. According to this Covenant, God has promised His guidance and blessings to humanity by means of the Prophets, such as Noah, Abraham, Jesus, and Bahá'u'lláh. Other Envoys of God will come in future ages also, as long as man exists, to guide us on the spiritual path.

Mankind, as the other party of this supreme Covenant, must fulfill his role also. Having free will, man can choose his path: good or evil; truth or falsehood; the spiritual or the material; God or self. In the Person of the Prophet is manifested the full expression of the Will of God; therefore to accept or reject the Prophet is the supreme and critical decision of man. Through acceptance of the Prophet, through following and dedicating oneself to Him, through sacrificing personal well-being and accepting adversities, man fulfills the foremost responsibility of his existence. In this way man is faithful to the Eternal Covenant.

God has sent the Prophets who have come to the world in fulfillment of the Eternal Covenant. Since the twelve tribes of Israel represent the succession of Divine Revelations, they also represent the Eternal Covenant, which is the foundation upon which progressive revelation unfolds.

We have referred before to another Covenant, that of Bahá'u'lláh, which contains explicit instructions for His followers to turn to 'Abdu'l-Bahá after His death. The Covenant of Bahá'u'lláh has authority for Bahá'ís as a result of having accepted Bahá'u'lláh as the Messenger of God for this age, in recognition that Bahá'u'lláh again fulfills the Eternal Covenant of God. In this sense, the Covenant of Bahá'u'lláh (the Lesser Covenant) is a fruit and a result of the Eternal Covenant (the Greater Covenant). We have already mentioned the transcendental role of the Covenant of Bahá'u'lláh in protecting the unity of the Bahá'í Faith and thus assuring that this Revelation will bear the fruits latent within it. This same unity, built upon the foundation of the Lesser Covenant, is its greatest fruit, in that it overcomes the differences of race, class, nationality and religion which divide humanity today. Some day in the future, the world will find itself obligated to adopt this example of unity to resolve the problems which are destroying its very life.

The theme of the Covenant and its symbolic representation in the tribes of Israel will be critical in order to understand the prophecy of Revelation which speaks of the twelve tribes.

In Revelation, we see that the twelve tribes are to be restored in twelve equal groups of twelve thousand each, for a total of 144,000.

"Of the tribe of Judah were sealed twelve thousand. Of the tribe of Reuben were sealed twelve thousand. Of the tribe of Gad were sealed twelve thousand. Of the tribe of Aser were sealed twelve thousand. Of the tribe of Nepthalim were sealed twelve thousand. Of the tribe of Manasses were sealed twelve thousand. Of the tribe of Simeon were sealed twelve thousand. Of the tribe of Levi were sealed twelve thousand. Of the tribe of Issachar were sealed twelve thousand. Of the tribe of Zabulon were sealed twelve thousand. Of the tribe of Joseph were sealed twelve thousand. Of the tribe of Benjamin were sealed twelve thousand." (Rev. 7:5-8)

In Genesis the twelve tribes of Israel represent the Eternal Covenant of God. Insomuch as the 144,000 are derived from the twelve tribes, we suggest that these represent the Covenant of Bahá'u'lláh, which is derived from the Eternal Covenant. The following is a discussion of this hypothesis.

If in Genesis the twelve tribes represent progressive revelation and a succession of Divine Dispensations, then the unification of the tribes in Revelation represents the unification of the peoples and religions in the last days. In one sense this could be the union of the followers of the diverse creeds into one universal religion, but we have already seen that this union involves a "multitude" without number who will be drawn from "the nations and tribes and peoples" of the world. The 144,000 are independent of the multitude, and this suggests that the unification implicit in the election of the 144,000 has a more profound significance; these should be a focal point of that spiritual unity. 'Abdu'l-Bahá tells us that the Covenant of Bahá'u'lláh is "the axis of the unity of human kind"[7], the foundation itself of its spiritual unity. Therefore, the 144,000 must be directly related with the Covenant of Bahá'u'lláh.

In so much as the twelve tribes represent the Eternal Covenant manifested throughout history in successive revelations and religions, the 144,000 are derived from that Covenant and are summed from among those religions. 'Abdu'l-Bahá speaks of the Covenant of Bahá'u'lláh in the same terms, in relation with the revelations of the past, saying that it is "the *sum of all sacred writings*, ancient and modern"[8]. That is, all the religions find in the Lesser Covenant the fulfillment of their highest aspirations.

The Covenant of Bahá'u'lláh was manifested first in the Person of 'Abdu'l-Bahá and later in the Bahá'í Administrative Order which includes the Guardianship. Today, the Universal House of Justice is the supreme body of the Administrative Order and the bearer of the standard of the Covenant. In a more specific sense, the 144,000 represent the Universal House of Justice.

The Universal House of Justice, as the focal point of the Covenant today, represents a transcendental step in the progress of humanity, a true fruit of its spiritual and social evolution. It is impossible to find among the religious and secular institutions of the world, another that is elected by universal suffrage with the participation of persons of all social classes; that functions on a world level at the head of a community that includes more than 2,000 national and ethnic groups; whose *modus operandi* is not coercion and oppression, but love and justice; and whose purpose is the well being not only of its own adherents, but of humanity in general. Taking these aspects of the Universal House of Justice into account, we may well consider it as a herald of a new stage in human progress. The Universal House of Justice, manifestation of the Covenant of Bahá'u'lláh, is one of the foremost fruits of His Revelation and offers to humanity a model of the integration and unity for which it longs. The Universal House of Justice is the greatest hope which the world has today, an institution which is unique in history.

Another prophecy related to that of the 144,000 in Revelation is found in the Old Testament. Speaking of the destiny of the Jews in the last days, when they will be rescued from the foreign lands where they would pass their exile, the prophet Zephaniah says:

"In that day shalt thou not be ashamed for all thy doings, where in thou has transgressed against me: for then I will take away out of the midst of thee them that rejoice in thy pride, and thou shalt no more be haughty because of my holy mountain. I will also leave in the midst of thee an afflicted and poor people, and they shall trust in the name of the Lord. The remnant of Israel shall not do iniquity, nor speak lies; neither shall a deceitful tongue be found in their mouth." (Zep. 3:11-13).

This prophecy bears great similarity to those of Revelation with respect to the 144,000. First, there is reference to the "remnant of Israel", in accord with the election of the 144,000 from among the tribes of Israel. Second, the remnant of Israel will not "speak lies, neither shall a deceitful tongue be found in their mouth." This is almost identical to what is said about the 144,000 in Rev. 14:5. Thirdly, Zephaniah refers to the "holy mountain", and in Rev. 14:1 we read that the 144,000 are manifested on the holy mountain, Mount Zion. From this evidence we conclude that the prophecy of Zephaniah refers to the same 144,000 of Revelation.

What we learn additionally in Zephaniah 3 is that the "remnant of Israel", or the 144,000, are to manifested "in the midst" of the Jews returned to the Holy Land. This belies what some propose that the 144,000 are the members of this or that sect scattered throughout the world. Rather, the 144,000 are to be established in the Holy Land, "in the midst" of the Jews.

We can compare the prophecy of Zephaniah with one of Bahá'u'lláh in the Tablet of Carmel. Again, addressing Mount Carmel, Bahá'u'lláh says:

The Throne of God

"Ere long will God sail His Ark upon thee, and will manifest the people of Bahá who have been mentioned in the Book of Names."[9]

Here, too, in the Tablet of Carmel, there is mention of God's holy mountain, as there is in Zephaniah 3. The Ark which is to sail upon the holy mountain is the Ark of the Covenant, here compared implicity with the Ark of Noah which was a refuge and shelter for humanity. As in Zephaniah 3, Bahá'u'lláh also refers to a "people" which will be manifested, "the people of Bahá", which is the Universal House of Justice. To these Bahá'u'lláh promised His guidance, assuring that they would indeed speak the truth, as foreseen in Zephaniah and Revelation. The prophecy of Bahá'u'lláh has been fulfilled in this century, and the Universal House of Justice is now manifest upon Mount Carmel, "in the midst" of the Jews returned to the Holy Land.

The prophecy of Bahá'u'lláh with respect to the Covenant and the Universal House of Justice bears great similarity to the prophecy of Zephaniah and the latter evidently refers to the same 144,000 of Revelation.

The Universal House of Justice, represented as the 144,000, has its seat on Mount Carmel, which has been designated as the throne of God in this world. We have seen that the Lamb (the Báb) has His Sanctuary in the vicinity of the throne (Mount Carmel) and the 144,000 are together with Him.

"... and lo, a Lamb stood on the Mount Zion ..... and with him an hundred forty and four thousand." (Rev. 14:1)

In other verses, we find confirmation that the 144,000 are in the vicinity of the throne; for we read:

"And they sung as it were a new song before the throne." (Rev. 14:3)

"... (and are) without fault before the throne of God." (Rev. 14:5)

So we see that the 144,000 (Universal House of Justice) are also found at the throne (Mount Carmel), as is the case in reality.

We noted before a relationship between the Promised Law of God and the 144,000, due to the proximity of these to Mount Zion, which is the origin of the law in the latter days. The Universal House of Justice is the only institution of the Bahá'í Faith explicitly authorized by Bahá'u'lláh to formulate laws according to the needs of future ages. Also, we saw that the rainbow, ancient symbol of the Covenant, is spread out about the throne (Rev. 4:3), a prophecy fulfilled with the manifestation of the Covenant on Mount Carmel.

In summary, in our modern epoch, the unification of the tribes of Israel represents the unification of the religions of the world, that is, the spiritual unification of humanity. The mechanism for the establishment of the spiritual unity is the Covenant of Bahá'u'lláh, of which the Universal House of Justice is now the focal point. Therefore, the Universal House of Justice

The Throne of God

is represented in Revelation as the 144,000, in recognition of its central role in establishing the spiritual unity of mankind. The relationships among the several prophecies in this chapter are summarized in Figure 4.

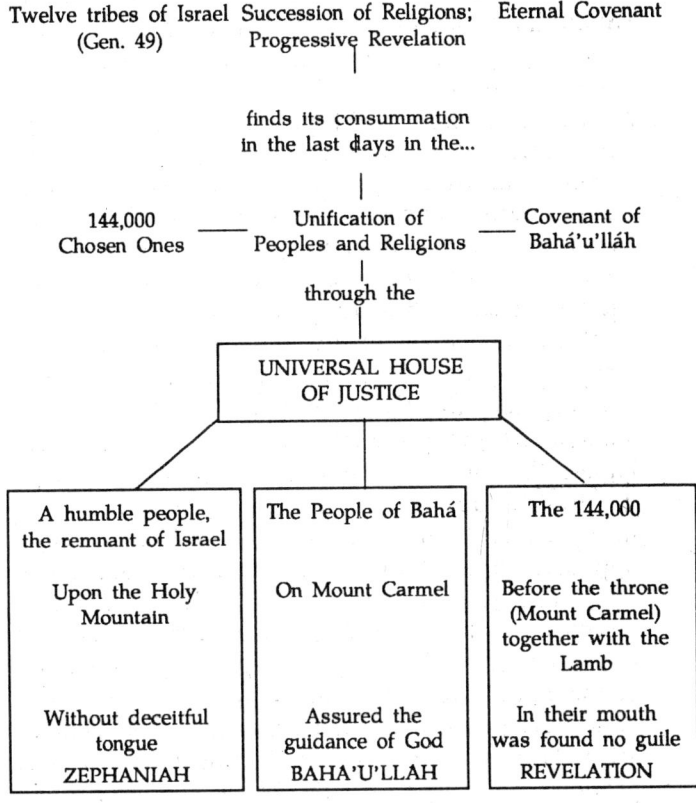

Figure 4. A Summary of the Prophecies Related to the 144,000 Chosen Ones of Revelation

REFERENCES

1. Bahá'u'lláh, *Gleanings from the Writings of Bahá'u'lláh* p. 15.
2. 12:3.
3. 12:7.
4. In his work *The Apocalypse Unsealed*, the author, Robert Riggs notes a symbolic connection of the twelve tribes of Genesis 49 with the signs of the Zodiac and specifically, Judah with Leo the Lion. 'Abdu'l-Bahá, in turn, compared the revelation of Bahá'u'lláh with the sign of Leo in the sense that it is the sign when the sun is in its zenith (*God Passes By*, p. 99).
5. As we have cited in the previous note, Mr. Riggs has connected the tribes of Genesis 49 with the Zodiac and Gad with the sign of Aries. Again, 'Abdu'l-Bahá compared the sign of Aries with the Revelation of the Báb, in that Aries is the first sign in which "the sun enters at the vernal equinox" (*God Passes By*, p. 99).
6. A close connection exists between the stories of Joseph, the Imám Husayn and Bahá'u'lláh. In His masterpiece, the Qayyumul-Asma', the Báb has associated Joseph with Husayn and also with Bahá'u'lláh and compared the suffering of Joseph in the hands of his brothers with those of Bahá'u'lláh, whose brother was His greatest opposer. Bahá'u'lláh and Husayn are both called "the true Joseph" (*God Passes By*, p. 23; and *Selections from the Writings of the Báb*, p. 49). On the other hand, Bahá'u'lláh represents the return of the Imám Husayn awaited by the Shi'ahs (*God Passes By*, p. 94) and Bahá'u'lláh identified Himself with Husayn, among other major and minor prophets (*Gleanings from the Writings of Bahá'u'lláh*, p. 95). The Báb, alluding to Bahá'u'lláh's own name (which was Husayn 'Alí), refers to Him as

The Throne of God

the Son of 'Alí (Imám Ḥusayn). Therefore, the interpretation of the Joseph of Genesis 49:22 as Ḥusayn can be extended to Bahá'u'lláh also, above all because the Cause of Ḥusayn was vindicated with the coming of Bahá'u'lláh, as is implicit in the promise for the last days of the blessing and multiplying of this Joseph, till the "everlasting hills".

7. 'Abdu'l-Bahá, *Tablets of the Divine Plan*, p. 21.
8. 'Abdu'l-Bahá, quoted in *The Covenant of Bahá'u'lláh;* p. 72.
9. Bahá'u'lláh, *Gleanings from the Writings of Bahá'u'lláh*, p. 16 (XI).

CHAPTER 18

Armageddon

Armageddon is a topic which occupies the attention of thousands of Christians. Many are convinced that the battle of Armageddon is imminent. Furthermore, 'Abdu'l-Bahá said in 1912, shortly before the First World War,
> "We are on the eve of the Battle of Armageddon referred to in the sixteenth chapter of Revelation. The time is two years hence, when only a spark will set aflame the whole of Europe."[1]

These words of 'Abdu'l-Bahá do not necessarily mean that Armageddon has passed, but that it began in 1914 with the First World War which was only "the first stage in a titanic convulsion"[2]. In one sense, Armageddon represents all the wars, social struggles and disorder which have shaken the whole world in this twentieth century. The wars are only the most visible and destructive signs of the chaos of a world going through changes which it can neither control nor direct.

Assuming that Armageddon began with the First World War, it is interesting to speculate why the Bible has designated the disorders of the twentieth century with the name of *armageddon*.

If we put ourselves in the place of the ancient prophets looking to the future, it would have been impossible to explain the struggles of the twentieth century in terms of the European countries which have been the principle participants in the wars. They did not exist in the Prechristian Era, nor for many years after Christ. Instead, the prophets referred to these wars and disorders (beginning with the First World War) in terms of places known to the Jews and the early Christians. Armageddon usually is related to the Valley of Megiddo in Israel and it was there that the decisive battle of the First World War in the Middle Eastern theater took place, between the English and Turkish forces.

It was the 19th of September, 1918, that the British Commander, General Allenby, advancing from Egypt on the south, commanded his cavalry to charge the enemy line, dividing the Turkish army and opening the road to Damascus[3]. This occurred in the battle of Megiddo. Thus it is that in context of the Middle East, the battle of Megiddo (or Armageddon) represents the First World War and marks the beginning of this period of chaos and wars.

Although the Bahá'í Writings foretell even more suffering for humanity, they also contain a promise of hope for the future and a firm conviction that peace is inevitable[4]. 'Abdu'l-Bahá predicted that world peace would be established within this twentieth century.

It is also interesting to review the historical events of the battle of Megiddo in the light of the book of Ezekiel. We note that Gog and Magog, the prince and the kingdom whose defeat was promised in Armageddon, came from the north (Ez. 38-39). The Turkish forces which were defeated in the battle of Megiddo also came from the north.

In this same chapter of Ezekiel we find a reference to the forces of good which will struggle against Gog. According to Ezekiel, in the battle of Megiddo Sheba and Dedan will participate:

"Sheba, and Dedan, and the merchants of Tarshish, with all the young lions thereof, shall say unto thee, Art thou come to take a spoil? has thou gathered thy company to take a prey....? (Ez. 38:13)

Sheba and Dedan were ancient cities in the prechristian time and it appears that they would help God in this battle. However, these cities had ceased to exist for centuries. Then to what do these names refer?

Sheba and Dedan were also descendants of Abraham through His wife Keturah and His son, Jokshan (Gen. 25:1-3). Some British Israelites in the past century interpreted this to mean that the Messiah of the last days that would come to defeat the forces of evil would be a descendant of Abraham through Keturah[5]. In fact, the lineage of Bahá'u'lláh traced to Abraham and Keturah[6], and Bahá'u'lláh and His own Son, 'Abdu'l-Bahá fulfilled these expectations.

The battle of Megiddo has a special significance in the history of the Bahá'í Faith also. During the war, 'Abdu'l-Bahá was threatened by the commander of the Turkish forces in Haifa, who had sworn to crucify Him on Mount Carmel and destroy the Sanctuary of Bahá'u'lláh before abandoning the city. However, the English troops advanced so rapidly that the Turks fled without time to think of other things. On September 23, only four days after the battle of Megiddo began, the English captured Haifa and 'Abdu'l-Bahá was safe[7]. Sheba and Dedan could well challenge Gog saying "has thou gathered thy company to take a prey...?" The battle of Megiddo was not only the defeat of Gog and Magog (the Turks), but also the liberation of the descendants of Abraham, 'Abdu'l-Bahá and His family, and also of the Sanctuary of Bahá'u'lláh.

We have said that in the broad sense, Armageddon represents the wars and social struggles of this twentieth century, beginning with the First World War. But in a more specific sense, Armageddon has a special significance in the defeat of Turkey and thus, in the divine chastisement of the Caliphate, which is one of the recurring themes of Revelation that we have previously discussed.

REFERENCES

1. 'Abdu'l-Bahá, quoted in *Bahá'u'lláh and the New Era* p. 243.
2. Shoghi Effendi, *God Passes By* p. 305.

3. "World Wars", *Encyclopedia Brittanica*, 15th edition, vol. 19 (Macropaedia), p. 964.
4. Universal House of Justice, *The Promise of World Peace*, p. 1.
5. William Sears, op. cit., pp. 227-229.
6. Shoghi Effendi, *God Passes By*, p. 94.
7. Ḥasan Balyuzi, *'Abdu'l-Bahá*, p. 375.

CHAPTER *19*

A Miniature Book of Revelation: Matthew 24

We have established a chronology of the events described in Revelation and we have seen that the future events (from the point of view of a Christian in the first century) are related to the fifth, sixth and seventh stages. It is interesting to compare this chronology with another chapter of the Bible widely quoted in connection with the return of Christ, which is Matthew 24.

This chapter is especially appropriate for such an analysis for two reasons. First, because it constitutes the answer which Jesus gave to His disciples when they asked Him:

"... when shall these things be? and what shall be the sign of thy coming, and of the end of the world?" (Mat. 24:3)

Since the disciples have asked "WHEN" He would come, we should suppose that the answer that Jesus gave them should be adequate to responding to this question and should lend itself to determining the specific time of the return.

Second, the answer which Jesus gave appears to be a description of events in chronological order, because Jesus punctuated His response saying "Then...", "Afterward...", etc. At times the signs of Mat. 24 are cited as isolated events, but if we study them in the order in which Jesus presented them, we will see a connection with the chronology of Revelation.

What, then, was the answer of Jesus? And how is it related to the 1,900 years of history since the time of Jesus?

First, Jesus tells of false prophets that will come announcing themselves as the Christ:

> "And many shall come in my name, saying, I am Christ; and shall deceive many." (Mat. 24:5)

This was fulfilled within a few years of the crucifixion. Among the Jews many leaders arose announcing themselves as the Christ, or the Messiah. In general, these aspired to a worldly sovereignty and sought to fulfill the expectations of the Jews for a militaristic Messiah, who would liberate his people from the Roman yoke.

> "And ye shall hear of wars and rumours of wars: ....For nation shall rise against nation, and kingdom against kingdom; and there shall be famines, pestilences, and earthquakes, in divers places. All these are the beginning of sorrows." (Mat. 24:6-8).

These words can be applied to almost any epoch of history, for humanity has never been free of these evils. In our chronology they could represent the wars perpetrated by the Romans, which finally destroyed Jerusalem, but the

A Miniature Book of Revelation: Matthew 24

description of Jesus seems broader in that He says "nation shall rise against nation and kingdom against kingdom". The subjection of the Jewish people by Imperial Rome cannot well be described as "kingdom against kingdom". These words apply better to that which occurred in the time of Muḥammad and in Revelation we see that the epoch of Muḥammad was foretold as a time of wars (Rev. 9). The Moslems under the Sunni Caliphs carried on a campaign of conquest which created an empire larger even than that of Rome.

> "Then shall they deliver you up to be afflicted, and shall kill you: and ye shall be hated of all nations for my name's sake." (Mat 24:9)

Although every religion has had heroes and martyrs, we proposed that the martyrs named in Revelation are of the epoch of Muḥammad (Rev. 6:9, 20:4). We saw in Revelation 13 and 20 that Ḥusayn in particular occupies an important place in the Biblical prophecies about martyrs. In so much as Jesus has prophesied martyrs in Mat. 24, the prophecies would be consistent if they referred to the same martyrs.

> "And many false prophets shall rise, and shall deceive many." (Mat. 24:11)

Is this a only a repetition of the previous warning in Mat. 24:5, or does it represent a new step in the chronology? We are seeing that the words of Jesus can refer to the events of the Dispensation of Muḥammad. In this case the "false prophets" may be those Caliphs who opposed the Imáms and propagated the doctrine of the Sunni sect, which came to represent the majority in Islám: "and (they) shall deceive many".

"And this gospel of the kingdom shall be preached in all the world for a witness unto all nations; and *then shall the end come.*"

Traditionally this has been recognized as one of the most concrete signs of the return and it is especially significant because Jesus relates it directly with "the *end*". We might well ask ourselves, the end of *what*?

It is commonly supposed that this refers to the end of the world, according to the text of many Bibles. But in the translation of the New Testament from the Greek, "world" is derived from the word "Kosmos", which has two meanings. One is "the Universe", that is, the physical world, and the other is "cycle" or "epoch". Some modern students of the Bible have concluded that when Jesus spoke of the end of the *Kosmos,* He spoke of the end of an *epoch* (and the beginning of another!) Evidence to support this interpretation is that Jesus continued speaking of many signs and events which are to come after the "end" mentioned in Mat. 24:14. How would this be possible if the "end" were the end of the world? Furthermore, as for the sign of the end, that the Gospel would be preached in "all the world", this is a reality of our modern age and if the world still has not come to an end, apparently this is not the meaning of the prophecy.

A Miniature Book of Revelation: Matthew 24

Considering that the Gospel has already been taught in "all the world, for a testimony to all nations" (it may be prohibited in some countries to teach Christianity at this moment, but all the countries of the world have heard this, "testimony" at some time), then at what time was this sign fulfilled? The historians of the church note a surge of Evangelistic fervor in the first years of the past century which carried the Christian message to the countries of Africa and Asia, the last to receive the Evangel[1]. In reality, the fervor of the pastors was increased by the consciousness that they were fulfilling that sign of the coming of the Lord. While it would be arbitrary to fix an exact year for its fulfillment, we can cite the period of 1840 to 1850 as critical for this sign.

This coordinates very well with other prophecies which we have cited that indicate the year 1844 as the year of the advent.

Immediately after the prophecy of the universal proclamation of the Gospel and the coming of the end, Jesus gave another very specific sign of His return that is very significant in our chronology.

> "When ye therefore shall see the abomination of desolation, spoken of by Daniel the prophet, ... (whoso readeth, let him understand) (Mat. 24:15)

The prophecy of Daniel to which Jesus refers is found in Daniel 8:13 and contains a calculation of years based on the period of 2,300 days (which is the equivalent of 2,300 years). A detailed explanation of this prophecy is found in the appendix of this book. Briefly, this period began in 457 B.C. with the edict of Artaxerxes, king of Persia and ended in 1844 A.D., year repeatedly indicated in the Biblical prophecies.

Christians frequently quote that which Jesus says later in this chapter, "of that day and hour knoweth no man", to say that is impossible to know when the Lord will come. However, it should be noted that Jesus said that no one knows "the day and the hour", but He does not say that no one knows the *year*. Furthermore, insomuch as Jesus directed His disciples specifically to the prophecies of Daniel which contain a calculation of time and of these prophecies said, "whoso readeth, let him understand", one would suppose that it is possible to decipher and understand these calculations of the time of the return.

In terms of our chronology, it is significant that Jesus has mentioned in immediate succession these two signs, that of the proclamation of the Gospel and that of Daniel, in that the two were fulfilled in the same period. This is a confirmation that the events descrbied in Mat. 24 are in chronological order. Also, they give us a point of reference: 1844, the year of the advent of the Báb. Thus, the events described immediately afterward should be in reference to the Dispensations of the Báb and of Bahá'u'lláh.

"... then shall be great tribulation, such as was not since the beginning of the world to this time, no, or ever shall be." (Mat. 24:21)

A Miniature Book of Revelation: Matthew 24

We have already referred to the tribulation which occurred immediately after the Declaration of the Báb in 1844. The Shi'ah Moslems, incited by the priests, rose up against the Báb and massacred twenty thousand of His followers. One Austrian official, Captain Von Goumens, in the service of the Persian army, was witness of the atrocities which the Babis suffered[2]. In all his years of soldiering he had never seen such cruelty and suffering. Although trained with iron discipline for the rigors of the battlefield, that official renounced his post in disgust and returned to Europe.

> "And except those days should be shortened, there should no flesh be saved: but for the elect's sake those days shall be shortened." (Mat. 24:22)

The tribulation which overcame the Báb and His followers was of short duration but was furious. Almost all the Babi leaders perished in this tempest. Bahá'u'lláh was imprisoned and suffered several attempts against His life, but finally He was freed and banished from Persia. Bahá'u'lláh Himself was among the "elect" who came out of the "great tribulation".

> "Then if any man shall say unto you, Lo, here is Christ, or there; believe it not. For there shall arise false Christs and false prophets." (Mat. 24: 23, 24)

Far from being merely another warning of Jesus to His disciples against false prophets, this corresponds to the historical events of the Babi

Faith after the "great tribulation". The Báb had promised, after Him, another Prophet, "He whom God will make manifest". The few Babis that remained after the massacre in Persia were confused and dishertened. Many fled to Iráq for safety and there formed a small community. From among the Babis there arose at least twentyone "false prophets", declaring themselves to be that promised one[3]. Some had good intentions and others selfish motives, but none could give new life to the Cause of the Báb.

> "For as the lightning cometh out of the east, and shineth even unto the west; so shall also the coming of the Son of man be." (Mat. 24:27)

On one hand, Jesus is saying that the coming of the Son of Man will be dramatic an unmistakable compared with the multitude of "false prophets" which are to come. So it was that when Bahá'u'lláh arrived to Baghdád, in Iráq, His mere presence galvanized the Babi community. Although He did not make known His Divine Mission for ten years (until 1863), in the course of this period many came to the conclusion that He was the Promised One of the Báb. None could equal His wisdom and knowledge and many have left stories of their mystical experiences in His presence. During this period Bahá'u'lláh came to be the recognized Leader of the Babis without ever claiming this spiritual authority.

On the other hand, in the previous verse (Mat. 24:27), Jesus appears to be referring as

A Miniature Book of Revelation: Matthew 24

well to the route of Bahá'u'lláh in the course of His Banishment. He says He will come as the lightning, "from the east ... to the west". Why does Jesus say this, if it is not because the Son of Man is to come from the east? Lightning can fall from whatever part of the sky - not only in the east - and its light radiates in all directions, not only to the west. Rather, we know that Bahá'u'lláh came from the east (Persia) and traveled towards the west, first to Baghdád and later to Palestine.

"Immediately after the tribulation of those days shall the sun be darkened, and the moon shall not give her light, and the stars shall far from heaven, and the powers of the heavens shall be shaken." (Mat. 24:29)

We have repeated several times that the signs in the heavens refer to events in the domain of religion. The sun represents God, or the Messenger of God and the moon and stars are the priests, the lesser lights of the religion. When a religion is in decadence, when its spirit is dead and its followers seek only worldly benefits, it is said that the sun has become darkened, that is to say, the light of God is obscured. So was the religion of Moses when Jesus came and so also the religion of Muḥammad when the Báb and Bahá'u'lláh appeared. Indeed it is the very opposition that the previous religion presents to the New Message, that causes it to become darker still.

To say that "the moon shall not give her light" means that the priests will lose their power and no longer will be a source of light (Divine Knowledge). When Bahá'u'lláh arrived in Baghdád, the nearby cities of Karbila and Najaf were centers of Shi'ah theology. The priests were jealous of Bahá'u'lláh, but did not dare confront Him publicly, knowing that they could not equal His knowledge. In the face of the new sun of Bahá'u'lláh, the light of the moon was insignificant.

In one Tablet, Bahá'u'lláh declares that God has taken away the power of the priests in this day[4]. In reference to the fall of the stars, He states that this occurred when He was in banishment to Adrianople, in Turkish Europe[5].

"And then shall appear the sign of the Son of man in heaven: and then shall all the tribes of the earth mourn, and they shall see the Son of man coming in the clouds of heaven with power and great glory." (Mat. 24:30)

At last the Son of Man is in plain view of all. Possibly Jesus is referring to the Declaration of Bahá'u'lláh on April 21, 1863, when He made known His Mission to the Babi community, but insomuch as Jesus says that "all the tribes of the earth (shall) mourn", it rather appears that this refers to Bahá'u'lláh's public Declaration, made from Adrianople, when He made His call to the kings of the earth, ordering them to abandon the accumulation of armaments and to establish justice.

To say that the Son of Man will come in the "clouds of heaven" is another use of the symbols

A Miniature Book of Revelation: Matthew 24

which we have discussed. As the sun represents the Messenger of God, the clouds are things which hide the glory of the sun from the view of men. All the Messengers of God have come with great glory, not a mundane and obvious glory, but a spiritual glory. Each one has suffered persecution, has lived in poverty and has been humiliated. For men, this condition of the Prophets has been the cause of doubts, because men always expect the Prophets to come with an evident splendor. Therefore, the poverty and humiliation of the Prophets have been called "clouds", because to the sight of men, they hide the glory of the Prophet. We know that this was the cause for which the Jews rejected Jesus and it always has been a test which God has put to men, to recognize His Messengers for Their true glory.

> "And he shall send his angels with a great sound of a trumpet, and they shall gather together his elect from the four winds, from one end of heaven to the other." (Mat. 24:31)

The Babi community fell into a state of confusion when Bahá'u'lláh was banished from Baghdád to Constantinople, to Adrianople, and to the Holy Land. Many in Persia had not yet received the news of the Declaration of Bahá'u'lláh and His followers still did not know where He was or if He had died, due to the poor means of communication in those days. Bahá'u'lláh sent trusted teachers to Persia to revive the Babi community and to convey to them the remarkable news of the fulfillment of the promise of the Báb. The great majority accepted Bahá'u'lláh as that Promised One and at that time began to consider themselves as "Bahá'ís".

In a broader sense, this process continues today. The Bahá'í teachers, the angels of Bahá'u'lláh, carry His Message to the most remote corners of the globe, gathering "together his elect" from among all races, nations, and creeds.

> "Verily I say unto you, This generation shall not pass, till all these things be fulfilled." (Mat. 24:34)

Here Jesus refers to the generation of the time of the Báb and says that all these events will transpire within the life of that generation. The Báb's Mission initiated in 1844 and all the events of which we have written occurred in the course of the nineteenth century, before the death of Bahá'u'lláh in 1892. Certainly, many of the generation of the Báb and Bahá'u'lláh were witnesses of all these events.

This comment of Jesus reminds us of the passages of Revelation which also promise a rapid succession of events in the days of the Báb and Bahá'u'lláh[6]; for example: "The second woe is past; and, behold, the third woe cometh quickly".

"But as the days of Noah were, so shall also the coming of the Son of Man be. For as in the days that were before they were eating and drinking, marrying and giving in marriage, until

A Miniature Book of Revelation: Matthew 24

the day that Noah entered into the Ark, and knew not until the flood came, and took them all away; so shall also the coming of the Son of Man be." (Mat. 24:37-39)

In these words, Jesus carries the prophetic chronology beyond the coming of the Son of Man and speaks of a calamity which is to come after the return. We know that this calamity is different from the great tribulation mentioned in Matthew 24:21, for two reasons.

First, we saw that the tribulation of Mat. 24:21 was a tribulation which overcame the "elect", because if those days had not been shortened, all of the elect would have disappeared. On the contrary, the calamity which Jesus mentions here in Mat. 24:37 is a punishment for humanity in general, because it falls upon those who are submerged in the pleasures of eating, drinking, and marrying.

Second, it is obvious by the order of the events that the "great tribulation" occurs before the coming of the Son of Man, but by the very example which Jesus Himself gave, we see that this calamity appears after the coming. Jesus compares this calamity with that of the days of Noah, relating how Noah came, how the people rejected Him because they were immersed in mundane pleasures, how afterwards the deluge came as a punishment and only then did the people understand that Noah had spoken the truth. The implication is that at the coming of the Son of Man, the people will also reject Him due to indifference and as a consequence, a calamity will appear which will awaken them to reality.

Today many Christians believe that the world is near to such a calamity, but if this is true, it means that the Son of Man has already come. *Because this calamity is not a sign of His near advent, but rather a consequence of His coming and of the rebelliousness of humanity.*

REFERENCES

1. William Sears, op. cit., p. 29-33.
2. Shoghi Effendi, *God Passes By*, p. 65.
3. Ibid., p. 125.
4. Ibid., p. 231.
5. Bahá'u'lláh, *Epistle to the Son of the Wolf*, p. 132.
6. See Chapter 8.

Conclusion

We began this study of Revelation by commenting on the diverse opinions which exist with respect to this book. Skeptics consider that Revelation is no more than imagination and mythology, while many students of religion insist upon a purely literal interpretation.

We have offered an unorthodox interpretation, but based firmly in a logical analysis, in a rational and systematic study. As in all fields of human activity, we have seen that the application of logic to the Book of Revelation has been highly productive.

This analytical method has revealed to us certain key points that are necessary for understanding Revelation. First, that the visions of Revelation are highly repetitive. The same events are represented various times with different symbols. Second, that we can organize the events of Revelation on the basis of seven stages which we have interpreted as seven epochs in the spiritual development of humanity, each epoch being related to a Major Prophet. This does not necessarily mean that these are the only Major Prophets that have come to the world, but that these seven, for some reason, have been chosen as representative of the spiritual process which we have called "progressive revelation".

The process of organizing the events of Revelation in seven stages can be compared with organizing dominos, one behind the other in a long row. Then, by touching one domino, all the others fall in turn. The Bahá'í Writings provide us the keys which, like touching the first domino, give the initial impulse to the process of interpretation and afterwards, the significances of other events become clear. The Bahá'í Writings explain the meaning of the period of 1,260 years, the woman that represents the Law of God, the great beast and the New Jerusalem. With these keys we can understand almost all the Book of Revelation.

We have also seen that a knowledge of Islám is necessary to understand Revelation. For the Western mind, it may be difficult to accept an explanation which goes beyond Christianity, which embraces Islám as well. However, the events of the history of Islám fit perfectly with the prophecies of Revelation. If logic leads us to the conclusion that Muḥammad and Islám were foretold in Revelation, we should accept this conclusion.

In regards to the relationship between the Bahá'í Faith and Revelation, we can point out the following:
1. It is very significant that the Bahá'í Writings have been capable of unravelling the mysteries of Revelation. This fact is a testimony to the divine inspiration of the Bahá'í Writings.
2. The Bahá'í Faith, just as Islám, has fulfilled the prophecies of Revelation. We can

mention the following:
(a) The Bahá'í Faith was born in 1844, year which was foretold by the prophecy of the 391 years (Rev. 11:13). This period began with the fall of Constantinople to the Turks in 1453 and ended in 1844 with the coming of the Báb.
(b) The year 1844 also was foretold by the period of 1,260 years, reference to which is repeated many times in Revelation. This period is measured by the Moslem calendar and coincides with 1844 of the Gregorian calendar.
(c) Furthermore, in the Moslem calendar, 1844 coincides with the end of the thousand years since the disappearance of the last Shi'ah Imám, the period foretold in Rev. 20:7 and commonly known as the Millennium.
(d) The year 1844 also coincides with the beginning of the return of the Jews to the Holy Land (Rev. 3:9). This event always has been an important sign of the return of Christ in the last days.
(e) Having returned to their Promised Land, today the Jews worship God at the "feet" of the Báb, reunited around his Sanctuary (Rev. 3:9).
(f) The Báb was the Gate. A reference to His name is found in Rev. 3:8: "Behold, I have set before thee an open door".
(g) It was through this Gate the Bahá'u'lláh entered: "I stand at the door and knock"

(Rev. 3:20).

(h) The name of Bahá'u'lláh means "The Glory of God" and is also mentioned in Revelation: "The city had no need of the sun, neither of the moon, to shine in it: for the Glory of God did lighten it" (Rev. 21:23).

(i) The first light of the religion of the Báb dawned in the region of the Euphrates, where "the way of the kings of the east (was) prepared" (Rev. 16:12). The Báb and Bahá'u'lláh came from Persia, to the east of the Euphrates.

(j) Bahá'u'lláh came from Persia as was indicated in the reference to the coming of Michael, "one of the chief princes" of Persia (Rev. 12:7, Dan. 10-13).

(k) With the coming of the Báb and Bahá'u'lláh we have seen the destruction of the Turkish Empire, foretold in the prophecies of Armageddon (Rev. 16:12). The final defeat of the Turks in the battle of Megiddo corresponds to that described in Ezekiel 38-39.

(l) The books are opened! (Rev. 20:12). Bahá'u'lláh has explained the symbols of the ancient holy books, including the Bible and Revelation itself, as we have seen in this study.

(m) Bahá'u'lláh is the Lord of the Vineyard (Rev. 14:19) and has come to harvest the fruit of the vine. Bahá'u'lláh established the seat of the Bahá'í Faith upon Mount

Conclusion

Carmel, whose name means the "Vineyard of God".

The student of prophecy should refer to the book *Thief in the Night* for a broad discussion of Biblical prophecies fulfilled by the Báb and Bahá'u'lláh. Some of these prophecies are summarized in appendix 1.

Considered as a whole, these prophecies constitute a powerful testimony to the Missions of these Twin Prophets of the modern era. But beyond the testimony of prophecy, there is another testimony to the Divine Mission of the Prophet, which is the testimony of the Prophet Himself. Moses declared Himself dramatically with word and deed, and Jesus proclaimed Himself to be the one promised by Moses. Bahá'u'lláh, speaking of His own Mission says:

"Lo! The Father is come, and that which ye were promised in the Kingdom is fulfilled! This is the Word Which the Son concealed, when to those around Him He said: "Ye cannot bear it now".[1]

"Verily, He Who is the Spirit of Truth is come to guide you unto all truth. He speaketh not as prompted by His own self, but as bidden by Him Who is the All-Knowing, the All-Wise. Say, this is the One Who hath glorified the Son and hath exalted His Cause. Cast away, O peoples of the earth, that which ye have and take fast hold of that which ye are bidden by the All-Powerful"[2].

Bahá'u'lláh declared Himself to be the Promised One named in innumerable Biblical passages and awaited by all the peoples of the world. In addition to references to Him by the Hebrew prophets, Zoroaster, ancient Prophet of Persia, foretold His advent as the coming of the "World-Savior Shah-Bahram". Buddha referred to Him when He promised a "Buddha named Maitreye, the Buddha of Universal Fellowship". The Bhagavad-Gita alluded to Him as the "Most Great Spirit", the "Tenth Avatar", the "Immaculate Manifestation of Krishna"[3].

Although this book is directed toward persons of a Christian tradition, not only will the Christian find in the Bahá'í Message the fulfillment of his highest aspirations, but the Moslem, the Jew, the Buddhist and the Hindu as well. Each religion has prophecies in common, each religion awaits the same Promised One and the corollary of this is that each religion shares the divine truth. This also is an explicit teaching of the Bahá'í Faith that engenders a respect and tolerance for all the great religions of the world. Furthermore, with the acceptance of Bahá'u'lláh, a person automatically accepts the other Prophets of the past. For example, the Jew, upon accepting Bahá'u'lláh as the Lord of Hosts, accepts Jesus as well; the Buddhist, when receiving the new Revelation, recognizes all the line of Hebrew Prophets. Thus, the ancient barriers constructed by human ignorance will crumble before the truth and humanity will inherit the unity so long denied.

With respect to the teachings the Bahá'u'lláh brought, more than one leader of thought of this century has discovered in the Bahá'í Message the light for which humanity is searching. We can quote the following examples[4]:

Dowager Queen Marie of Rumania:

"The Bahá'í teaching brings peace and understanding. It is like a wide embrace gathering together all those who have long searched for words of hope. It accepts all great prophets gone before, it destroys no other creeds and leaves all doors open. Saddened by the continual strife amongst believers of many confessions and wearied by their intolerance towards each other, I discovered in the Bahá'í teaching the real spirit of Christ so often denied and misunderstood: unity instead of strife, hope instead of condemnation, love instead of hate, and a great reassurance for all men.

"More than ever today when the world is facing such a crisis of bewilderment and unrest, must we stand firm in Faith seeking that which binds together instead of tearing asunder. To those searching for light, the Bahá'í Teachings offer a star which will lead them to deeper understanding, to assurance, peace and good will with all men."

Leo Tolstoy, Russian Writer:

"I... sympathize with Babiism with all my heart inasmuch as it teaches people brotherhood and equality and sacrifice of material life for service to God.

"The teachings of the Babis... have through

Bahá'u'lláh's teachings been gradually developed and now present us with the highest and purest form of religious teaching."

Helen Keller:
"The philosophy of Bahá'u'lláh deserves the best thought we can give it."

GEORGE WASHINGTON CARVER, North American Scientist:
"You hold in your organization the key that will settle all of our difficulties, real and imaginary."

LUTHER BURBANK, North American scientist:
"I am heartily in accord with the Bahá'í Movement, in which I have been interested for several years. The religion of peace is the religion we need and always have needed, and in this Bahá'í is more truly the religion of peace than any other."

THOMAS MASARYK, Founder and First President of the Republic of Czechoslovakia:
"Continue to do what you are doing, spread these principles of humanity and do not wait for the diplomats. Diplomats alone cannot bring the peace, but it is a great thing that official people begin to speak about these universal peace principles. Take these principles to the diplomats, to the universities and colleges and to other schools, and also write about them. It is the people who will bring universal peace."

It is our hope that you will also find in the Bahá'í Message the fulfillment of your most

Conclusion

cherished desires, and that this book will be only the beginning of your studies. If this is the case, we hope that you will contribute also to the establishment of those principles for which the Prophets sacrificed their lives, and that Bahá'u'lláh has announced again, in their most adequate form for the world today. There is no doubt that the world thirsts for the water of life, for lack of which we are seeing each day more of the disasters foretold in Revelation, to which Bahá'u'lláh also made reference.

How long will the world wait to put into practice the teachings which Bahá'u'lláh brought, and thus mitigate to some degree those disasters? We hope it will be soon.

REFERENCES

1. Bahá'u'lláh, *Tablets of Bahá'u'lláh*, p. 11.
2. Ibid., p. 12.
3. Shoghi Effendi, *God Passes By*, p. 95.
4. Universal House of Justice, *The Bahá'í World*, Vol. XIII, pp. 803-830.

Appendix 1

Other Biblical Prophecies Fulfilled in the Modern Era

1. We have commented on various prophecies which point to the year 1844 as the year of fulfillment and the year of the return of Christ. One of these prophecies is found in the book of Daniel and is connected with a prophecy of the first coming of Christ.

The prophet Daniel lived in the time of the exile of the Jews in Babylonia and later in Persia. The Jews of that period longed to return to the Holy Land, to build again the temple of Solomon and there to offer their sacrifices to the God of Israel. Daniel had two visions related to the return of the Jews and the rebuilding of the temple.

In the first vision which refers to the first coming of Christ, Daniel heard a voice saying:

"Seventy weeks are determined upon thy people and upon thy holy city, to finish the transgression, and to make an end of sins, and to make reconciliation for iniquity, and to bring in everlasting righteousness, and to seal up the vision and prophecy, and to anoint the most Holy." (Dan. 9:24)

In this case, "seventy weeks" are translated into 490 days, or 490 years, according to Biblical calculations (Ez. 4:6). In his vision, it was promised to Daniel 490 years from "the going forth of the commandment to restore and to build Jerusalem" (Dan. 9:25), until the time in which "shall Messiah be cut off" (Dan. 9:26), that is, until the crucifixion of Christ.

When was this edict given? There were really four edicts, but the first two remained unfulfilled. The third, of Artaxerxes, was carried out and the fourth, also of Artaxerxes, merely repeated what was said in the third and is an extension of the same. Then it is the third edict, given in 457 B.C. that interests us.

If we count 490 years forward from 457 B.C., we arrive at the year 33 A.D., the approximate year of the crucifixion: traditionally it is said that Jesus was 33 years old when He died. Thus we see that Daniel predicted with great precision the period from the edict of Artaxerxes until the crucifixion: 490 years.

The second vision of Daniel is related to the previous one and of it we read:

> "Then I heard one saint speaking, and another saint said unto that certain saint which spoke, How long shall be the vision concerning the daily sacrifice, and the transgression of desolation, to give both the sanctuary and the host to be trodden under foot? And he said unto me, Unto two thousand and three hundred days; then shall the sanctuary be

cleansed." (Dan. 8:13-14)

This prophecy speaks of a much longer period of time: 2,300 days (2,300 days 2,300 years).

These 2,300 years are described, first as a time of "continual sacrifice" and later, as a time of "transgression of desolation" when the sanctuary will be trodden under foot. The period of continual sacrifice refers to the time (still in the future when Daniel had the vision) in which the Jews would again be in the Holy Land offering sacrifices in the temple. We have seen that this time began with the edict of Artaxerxes in 457 B.C. Afterwards would come a period of desolation; a new banishment and long years of suffering. This came after the crucifixion of Christ. The total period covering all this long history would be 2,300 years and afterward the sanctuary would be purified.

If we count 2,300 years forward from 457 B.C. we arrive to the year 1844 A.D. confirming again the prophecies which show this year as that of the advent. In 1844, the Báb appeared to purify the sanctuary of the religion of God.

It is very significant that Jesus Himself referred to this prophecy when the disciples asked Him when He would come again. Jesus said:

> "When ye therefore shall see the abomination of desolation, spoken of by Daniel, the prophet, ... (whoso readeth, let him understand):

Furthermore, we can note that this period of 2,300 years began and ended with royal edicts: first, with an edict emitted by Artaxerxes, king of Persia, in 457 B.C.; and later, with the so-called Edict of Toleration signed by the Sultan of Turkey in 1844 A.D. (see Chapter 8). It is curious that each of these edicts had the same effect, that of permitting the Jews to return to the Holy Land after long exiles. Even more curious is that Bahá'u'lláh Himself arrived in the Holy Land in the same way: first, by an edict of the king of Persia ordering His exile from that country; and later, by an edict of the Sultan of Turkey, which carried Him to the prison of Akká.

2. It was foretold by the prophet Zechariah that in the last days there would be two Messengers. Referring to two olive branches which the prophet saw in his vision, we read:

> "And said he, These are the two anointed ones, that stand by the Lord of the whole earth. (Zec. 4:14)

The word "anointed" means a Christ or Messiah. The two anointed ones are the Báb and Bahá'u'lláh.

3. The Prophet Ezekiel saw the "Glory of God" in a vision, near the Chebar River (Ez. 3:23). The name of Bahá'u'lláh means the "Glory of God" and the Chebar River is found in Iráq, near Baghdád where Bahá'u'lláh spent ten years of banishment.

Afterward, Ezekiel saw that the "Glory of God" came to Israel from the East (Ez. 43:2), just as Bahá'u'lláh came to Israel from Persia, to the East of Israel.

4. In the book of Jeremiah, a divine sovereignty was promised to the country of Elam, which today is part of Irán:

> "And I will set my throne in Elam, and will destroy from thence the king and the princes, saith the Lord." (Jer. 49:38)

Elam corresponds to the south of Irán, where the Báb appeared in the city of Shiráz.

5. The Prophet Micah, speaking of the last days, said:

> "In that day also he shall come even to thee from Assyria, and from the fortified cities, and from the fortress even to the river, and from sea to sea, and from mountain to mountain. Not withstanding the land shall be desolate because of them that dwell therin, for the fruit of their doings. Feed thy rod, the flock of thine heritage, which dwell solitarily in the wood, in the midst of Carmel" (Micah 7:12-14).

This prophecy applies word for word to Bahá'u'lláh, because in His banishment from Persia to Israel, Bahá'u'lláh passed through Iráq (ancient Assyria) and by way of the mountains of Persia, Iráq and Turkey. He crossed the Black Sea and the Mediterranean Sea and sojourned in the fortified cities of Constantinople and 'Akká. In His last years He raised His tent upon Mount Carmel where He fed His flock with His word.

6. Just as Micah prophesied the coming of the Promised One of Mount Carmel, so did Isaiah also:

> "... the excellency of Carmel and Sharon, they shall see the glory of the Lord..." (Is. 35:2)

Again we note the relationship between the name of Bahá'u'lláh (The Glory of God) and the promise of the coming of the "Glory of the Lord."

Isaiah says that in the days of this prophecy the

desret "shall blossom like a rose" (Is. 35:1), a miracle associated with the modern era in which the deserts of Israel yield abundant crops of grains, vegetables, and fruits.

7. Other prophecies refer to the coming of a Redeemer to babylon, an ancient city whose ruins are found near the city of Baghdád where Bahá'u'lláh lived for a several years. Isaiah says:
> "The Lord hath loved him: he will do his pleasure on Babylon, and his arm shall be on the Chaldeans" (Is. 48:14).

Zechariah told of one called Zerubbabel, name which means "banished in Babylonia" or "engendered in Babylonia":
> "The hand of Zerubbabel has laid the foundation of this house" (Zec. 4:8).

Either interpretation of the name Zerubbabel can apply to Bahá'u'lláh, in that He truly was banished in Babylon and there He made public His Mission, that is to say, His Cause was "engendered in Babylon".

Also, Micah, who prophecied the coming of Bahá'u'lláh from Assyria, said that there would be an act of redemption in Babylonia:
> "... and thou shalt go even to Babylon; there shalt thou be delivered; and there the Lord shall redeem thee from the hand of thine enemies." (Micah 4:10)

Appendix 2
Bibliography

'Abdu'l-Bahá. *Some Answered Questions*. New Delhi: Bahá'í Publishing Trust, 1973.
'Abdu'l-Bahá. *The Secret of Divine Civilization*. Wilmette: Bahá'í Publishing Trust, 1970.
'Abdu'l-Bahá. *Selections from the Writings of 'Abdu'l-Bahá*. Haifa: Bahá'í World Center, 1978.
'Abdu'l-Bahá. *Tablets of the Divine Plan*. Wilmette: Bahá'í Publishing Trust, 1974.
Ameer Alí, Syed. *The Spirit of Islám. A History of the Evolution and Ideals of Islám with a Life of the Prophet*. London: Methuen and Co. Ltd. (University Paperbacks), 1965. London: Chatto and Windus Ltd. (Cased Edition).
The Báb. *Selections from the Writings of the Báb*. Haifa: Bahá'í World Center, 1976.
Bahá'u'lláh. *Epistle to the Son of the Wolf*. Wilmette: Bahá'í Publishing Trust, 1976.
Bahá'u'lláh. *The Book of Certitude*. Wilmette: Bahá'í Publishing Trust, 1970.
Bahá'u'lláh. *Gleanings from the Writings of Bahá'u'lláh*. Wilmette: Bahá'í Publishing Trust, 1971.
Bahá'u'lláh. *Tablets of Bahá'u'lláh*. Haifa: Bahá'í World Center, 1978.
Balyuzi, Ḥasan. *'Abdu'l-Bahá*. Oxford: George Ronald, 1973.
Balyuzi, Ḥasan. *Muḥammad and the Course of Islám*. Oxford: George Ronald, 1976.
Biblical Society of America. *The Bible*. 1960.
Blackstone, W.E. *Jesus Viene*. Miami: Editorial Vida, 1982.
Cobb, Stanwood. *Islamic Contributions to Civilization*. Washington D.C.: Avalon Press, 1963.
Esslemont, J.E. *Bahá'u'lláh and the New Era*. Wilmette: Bahá'í Publishing Trust, 1978.
Faizi, Abul-Qasím. *The Prince of Martyrs: a brief account of the Imám Ḥusayn*. Oxford, George Ronald, 1977.

Bibliography

Hamid'u'lláh, M. *Introduction to Islám.* 4th edition. Lahore: Ashraf Press, 1974.
International Bible House. *Holy Bible.* Wheaton: 1977.
Muḥammad. *The Koran.* Harmondsworth: Penguin Books, 1974.
Marsella, Elena Maria. *The Quest for Eden.* New York: Philosophical Library, 1966.
Moffet, Ruth J. *New Keys to the Book of Revelation.* New Delhi: Bahá'í Publishing Trust, 1977.
National Spirtual Assembly of the Bahá'ís of the British Isles. *The Covenant of Bahá'u'lláh.* London: Bahá'í Publishing Trust, 1963.
Riggs, Robert F. *The Apocalypse Unsealed.* New York: Philosophical Library, 1981.
Sears, William. *Thief in the Night.* Oxford: George Ronald, 1974.
Shoghi Effendi. *The Unfoldment of World Civilization.* in, *The World Order of Bahá'u'lláh.* Wilmette: Bahá'í Publishing Trust, 1974.
Shoghi Effendi. *The Promised Day is Come.* Wilmette: Bahá'í Publishing Trust, 1980.
Shoghi Effendi. *God Passes By.* Wilmette: Bahá'í Publishing Trust, 1970.
Shoghi Effendi. *The Dispensation of Bahá'u'lláh.* in, *The World Order of Bahá'u'lláh.* Wilmette: Bahá'í Publishing Trust, 1974.
Shoghi Effendi. *Dawn Breakers.* Wilmette: Bahá'í Publishing Trust, 1932.
Universal House of Justice. *Bahá'í World.* Volume XIII. Haifa: Bahá'í World Center, 1970.
Universal House of Justice. *Peace: a compilation.* Haifa: Bahá'í World Center, 1985.
Universal House of Justice. *The Promise of Peace.* Haifa: Bahá'í World Center, 1985.

Glossary

A.D.—after Christ; designates a solar year of the Gregorian calendar, beginning with the birth of Christ, although modern experts doubt the original calculations that established that date and initiated the calendar.

A.H.—after the Hegira; indicates a year of the Moslem lunar calendar beginning with the migration of Muḥammad from Mecca to Medina in 622 A.D.

Abbasid—dynasty of kings (Caliphs) whose seat was in Baghdád from 750 till 1258 A.D.; so named for their descendance from 'Abbas, uncle of Muḥammad.

Abdu'l-Bahá—eldest Son of Bahá'u'lláh. Designated as His successor. His given name was 'Abbas, but He took the title 'Abdu'l-Bahá (servant of the Glory) as evidence of His servitude to His Father.

Abu-Sufyan—leader of the house of Ummayad in Mecca during the life of Muḥammad and one of His principal opposers; father of Mu'awiyah, the first Ummayad Caliph.

Adhirbayjan—northwest province of Irán, boarding Turkey and the former Soviet Union.

Adrianople—city of European Turkey; capital of Ottoman Empire under Murad I (reigned 1360-1389).

Glossary

'Akká—fortified city on the Mediterranean coast of Palestine, known in the West as Acre from the Middle Ages when it was the capital of a Christian kingdom during the Crusades.

'Alí (Imám)—cousin of Muhammad and second to accept Him; recognized by the Shi'ah sect of Islám as His legitimate successor.

Annas—father-in-law to Caiaphas and one of the prominent Jews who condemned Jesus (John 18:13).

Armageddon—the final battle mentioned in Revelation between the forces of good and evil, commonly related with the great battle mentioned in Ez. 38 and in other Biblical passages.

Artaxerxes—king of Persia mentioned in the book of Ezra whose edict permitted Ezra to return to Jerusalem.

B.C.—Before Christ.

Báb—Title taken by Siyyid 'Alí Muhammad, founder of the Babi Faith. It is translated as "the gate."

Babylonia—Ancient power in the south of Mesopotamia and the Middle East for more than a thousand years, becoming Biblically important when, in the final years of the Empire, the king Nebuchadnezzar conquered Jerusalem in March, 597 B.C.

Baghavad Gita—one of the main holy books of the Hindus.

Baghdád—city in the valley of the Tigris River, founded by the Abbasid Caliph al-Mansur in 762 A.D. as his capital.

Bahá—in Arabic, literally, Glory or Splendor; in Bahá'í literature, it refers to Bahá'u'lláh.

Bahá'í—refers to the religion of Bahá'u'lláh; a follower of the same.

Bahá'u'lláh—title of Mirza Ḥusayn Alí, founder of the Bahá'í Faith. It means "Glory of God."

Bayan—major doctrinal book of the Bab, of nearly 8,000 verses. The central theme is the imminent advent of another Promised One.

Book of Certitude—book revealed by Bahá'u'lláh in two days and two nights in answer to questions from an uncle of the Báb about the Mission of the Báb. Here Bahá'u'lláh makes reference to the doctrine of progressive revelation and to the symbols of the Bible and the Qurán.

Caiaphas—Jewish high priest who condemned Jesus (John 18:13).

Caliph—literally, successor; it normally refers to the leader of the Sunni sect, that is, the sovereign of the Ummayad or 'Abbasid dynasty.

Carmel—mountain on the Mediterranean Coast of Palestine where the prophet Elias overcame the priests of Baal (I Kings 18).

Christ—title of Jesus which means "the anointed," which applies to the Messiah of the Jews.

Constantinople—literally, city of Constantine; seat of the Byzantine Empire and of the Eastern Orthodox Church from 330 when the Emperor Constantine established it as his capital, until 1453 when it fell under the Turks.

Glossary

Covenant—an agreement or contract. In the Bible, the Divine agreement between God and man, established through Noah and renewed by Abraham, Moses, and Jesus.

Dispensation—a period of time beginning with the coming of a Prophet, and during which the laws given by that Prophet are effective. A dispensation ends with the coming of another Prophet.

Edict of Toleration—an edict from the Sultan of Turkey emitted in 1844, under pressure from the European powers and principly the English, by which freedom of worship was permitted in the Ottoman Empire. Implicit in this edict was the permission for the Jews to return to the Holy Land.

Elias—Prophet of the Old Testament whose mission was to purify the religion of Jehovah of the foreign influences of the priests of baal (I and II Kings).

Euphrates—one of the two large rivers that cross the country of Iráq and enclose the region of Mesopotamia.

Guardianship—institution established by 'Abdu'l-Bahá in His Will and Testament, to which His grandson, Shoghi Effendi was named.

Haifa—city and principal port of Israel, on the Mediterranean Coast at the foot of Mount Carmel.

Hands of the Cause of God—in the Bahá'í Faith, a small group of persons who were named to this position in recognition of their erudition and spiritual stature, with responsibility of propagation and protection of the Bahá'í Faith.

Hejira—the migration of Muḥammad from Mecca to Medina in 622 A.D., which marked the beginning of the Moslem Calendar.

Hidden Imám—according to the Shi'ah belief, the twelfth and last Imám, who disappeared at the age of five and afterwards communicated with the Shi'ah faithful through four successive spokesmen.

Hijáz—the western region of Arabia, bordering the Red Sea, where Mecca and Medina are found.

Holy Land—in the context used in this book, Palestine.

Holy Spirit—the intermediary between God and His creation.

Ḥusayn (Imám)—grandson of Muḥammad and son of 'Alí, was the third in the line of successors to Muḥammad recognized by the Shi'ah sect.

Imám—one of the twelve hereditary successors of Muḥammad recognized by the Shi'ah sect. Although the title has been assumed by lesser leaders of Islám, here it refers only to those twelve.

Irán—Middle Eastern country which in the Bible is identified as Persia.

Iráq—Middle Eastern country whose territory includes Mesopotamia and that which was Babylonia and Assyria in ancient times.

Islám—religion founded by Muḥammad, literally means submission (to the will of God).

Ishmael—first son of the Prophet Abraham, born to the slave Hagar (Gen. 16:21).

Jehovah—Name of God in the Old Testament.

Glossary

Kaaba—literally, 'cube.' The center of Moslem worship in Mecca, supposedly constructed by Abraham.

Karbila—holy city on the Euphrates River in Iráq, where the tomb of the the Imám Ḥusayn is found.

Khadijah—first and only wife of Muḥammad until her death, the first person to believe in Him.

Kufah—city of the Euphrates valley where the Imám 'Alí was assassinated. This same city pledged its help to his son Ḥusayn, but later it betrayed him under pressure from the army of Yazid, the Ummayad Caliph.

Lunar year—year used in the Moslem Calendar, based on the phases of the moon, of 354 days per year. Due to having fewer days than the solar year, the anniversaries in the Moslem calendar change each year in relation with the respective dates in the Gregorian calendar.

Major Prophet—a Prophet chosen by God to begin an epoch, with authority to establish laws at His discretion, independent of previous Prophets.

Manifestation of God—in Bahá'í literature, one of the Major Prophets who reveal and manifest the perfections of God.

Mecca—sacred city of Islám in Arabia, where Muḥammad was born.

Medina—sacred city of Islám where Muḥammad was widely accepted for the first time as Prophet and where His Sanctuary is located.

Megiddo (Valley of)—plane in Palestine some 100 kilometers to the north of Jerusalem, supposedly the site of the great battle and the defeat of Gog and Magog in the last days.

Mesopotamia—literally, land between the rivers, refers to the region between the Euphrates and the Tigris where many civilizations of ancient times flourished.

Minor Prophets—a Prophet which derives his inspiration and authority from a Major Prophet.

Mírza Husayn 'Alí (1817-1892)—given name of Bahá'u'lláh, Founder of the Bahá'í Faith.

Moors—term applied to the Moslems of Spain, who were a mixture of Arabian, Spanish, and Berber bloods.

Mu'awiyah—son of Abu-Sufyan who rebelled against the Imám 'Alí, naming himself the first caliph of the Umayyad.

Muhammad—Prophet of Islám.

Moslem—follower of Islám, literally, one who submits (to the will of God).

Najaf—holy city of the Shi'ah sect in Iráq, it is the site of the sanctuary of 'Alí, first of the Imáms. Established by Harun-ar-Rashid in 791 A.D.

Ottoman—Empire born of a Turkish tribe that acquired importance in the Middle East in the XIV and XV centuries. At one time it included Egypt, Arabia, Palestine, Iráq, Turkey, and a good part of Eastern Europe.

Persia—ancient name for the country of Irán, the name being derived from the province of Fars.

Pharisee—one of the principle Jewish sects in the time of Jesus, characterized by their traditionalism and legalism.

Glossary

Progresive Revelation—doctrine according to which the Word of God is revealed to man gradually by means of successive Prophets in different ages.

Qa'im—the promised envoy of God awaited by the Shi'ah sect of Islám, whose coming is to bring the reign of peace and justice.

Quddus—the last of the eighteen disciples of the Báb to recognize Him, he held the highest spiritual position among the eighteen.

Qu'rán—the Holy book of Islám, which consists of verses revealed by the Prophet Muḥammad.

Religion—in the context used here, any of the great spiritual systems established by the Prophets of God, such as Christianity and Islám.

Revelation—the Word of God made known to man through the Prophets.

Sanctuary—temple where a religion venerates a holy personage; in the sense used here, in reference to the tomb itself.

Sasanid—last dynasty of the Persian kings before they were conquered by the Arabs in the seventh century; established in 224 A.D.

Sect—in the sense used here, any of the numerous divisions of the great religions of the past.

Shari'ah—codification of the Islamic law, accomplished in the eighth and ninth centuries, which applied the law of the Revelation of Muḥammad to private, social, religious, and political life.

Shaykh Ahmad (1744-1827)—founder of the Shaykhi sect, he taught a symbolic interpretation of the Qu'rán, declaring that the Promised One of Islám was soon to come.

Shi'ah—one of the two large branches of Islám, whose adherents believe in the succession of the Imams.

Shiráz—city in the south of Persia, famous for numerous mystic poets who have lived there; city of the birth of the Báb.

Shoghi Effendi (1897-1957)—great grandson of Bahá'u'lláh and grandson of 'Abdu'l-Bahá, was appointed Guardian of the Bahá'í Faith in the Testament of 'Abdu'l-Bahá.

Siyyid—a descendant of Muḥammad.

Siyyid 'Alí Muḥammad (1819-1850)—given name of the Báb, Founder of the Babi Faith.

Siyyid Kazim—a follower of Shaykh Ahmad, who became recognized as the leader of his disciples after his death.

Sultan—title of the Emperor of the Turkish Empire.

Tabarsi—name of a Moslem saint, whose sanctuary was converted into a fortress by the followers of the Báb who took refuge there.

Tablet—in the Bahá'í Faith, term that designates a sacred Epistle that contains a revelation.

Tihrán—capital of modern Iran.

Ummayad—one of the tribes of Mecca in the days of Muḥammad which was violently opposed to the Prophet. Later the Ummayad Caliphs seized the leadership of the nation of Islám in the days of the successors of Muḥammad.

Universal House of Justice—Supreme Administrative Body of the Bahá'í Faith, elected by universal suffrage, with its seat in Haifa, Israel.

Zion—one of the two mountains where ancient Jerusalem, the city of David, was situated. In its use in the Old Testament, Zion frequently substitutes for Jerusalem, and it figures in many prophecies, a place where Jehovah dwelled.